Microsoft Outlook 2000
Intermediate

Holly Freeman

Project Editor: Jennifer Jordan
Developmental Editor: Ron Pronk
Indexer: Lisa Probasco

Product code: 205–031400–PDF

ABOUT THIS BOOK

Essential Course Preparation Information

To match the TRY IT and SKILLCHECK exercises in this book, you should deactivate the "Menus show recently used commands first" option: click Tools on the menu bar, and click Customize on the Tools menu. Click the "Menus show recently used commands first" check box to clear it. You should also create a folder called "Outlook Intermediate" on each computer's hard disk. The students will use this folder to store any files created during class.

This book assumes that Outlook 2000 will be set up on classroom systems using the following default settings. Although the instructor may elect to change these defaults, doing so might alter the results of some instructions provided in this book. Students might also change the defaults during the course, which might alter the results for other students who use the same classroom systems. To ensure that changed settings do not affect classroom instruction, make sure that the following defaults are set before each class.

- The Inbox should be the default startup window. To set this, in the Outlook Today window click the Customize Outlook Today button and clear the When starting, go directly to Outlook Today check box.
- The Calendar view should be set to Day view.
- Maximize Outlook so that you can see as many buttons and options as possible.

After your class has worked through the exercises, you will have to delete or reset the following items (you might prefer to have students do this themselves at the end of class):

- Delete all messages that are in the Inbox.
- Delete all contact records.

- In Lesson 1, the students customize Outlook Today. You will have to restore it to its default settings. The students also assign various e-mail messages and a task to categories. You need to unassign these categories. The students also create and assign two categories called Picnic and Company Parties. (Display the Master Categories List and click the Reset button.)

- In Lesson 2, delete all tasks, appointments, and folders created. Delete student's names from the permission list, delegate list, and permissions list for Net Folder. Delete the OST file create on page 50. Delete the quick synchronization group called "Inbox/Cal/Contact." Restore the download options to the default. (Click Tools, point to Synchronize, click Offline Folder Settings, and click Download Options. In the Message size limit section, select 800, type the default number, and click OK twice.)

- In Lesson 3, delete the Cook Position folder and shortcut (which is on the Outlook bar). Delete the Attachments folder. Delete the "Cook" and "Attachments" rules. (Click Tools, click Rules Wizard, click the Click rule check box, click the Delete button, and click OK.) Delete the archive file from the Outlook Intermediate folder. Delete the signature called "Fun" and "Nickname." Delete the Personal Address book. Delete the personal distribution lists called "Marketing Department" and "Clients." Delete the templates called "Update" and "Weekly Repairs Report."

- In Lesson 4, restore the Calendar options to the default settings. Delete meetings. Delete multi-day events. Delete appointments or recurring appointments. In the Outlook Intermediate folder, delete the Web page Calendar folders called "Employee Volleyball" and "Basket Weaving Class."

- In Lesson 5, add and remove fields in the Show Fields dialog box as necessary, so that they match the fields displayed on page 169. Delete the Guest and Guest1 custom forms. (Refer to the TIP on page 178 to view the steps for deleting forms when Outlook is configured for Corporate or Workgroup.)

- In Lesson 6, delete tasks from the Tasks and Journal folders. Delete recurring tasks. Delete task requests.

Please note that Outlook 2000 remembers settings and tries to "learn" what features you want to use. As a result, some of the options in the classroom computers might already contain settings used in the previous class.

Using the Exercise Diskette

The files for all TRY IT and SKILLCHECK exercises are included on the exercise diskette.

The exercise diskette contains the following files and folders:

- Contacts (folder)
- Inbox (folder)
- Tasks (folder)
- Guests.mdb
- LMR Address List.mdb

To prepare for each class (and after performing the steps on the previous page), the contents of each folder must be replaced in Outlook. The documents **Guests** and **LMR Address List** will be accessed from the exercise diskette and should remain there. Prior to each class, it will be necessary to drag and drop the contents of the three folders—Contacts, Inbox, and Tasks—into Outlook. To do this, open Outlook 2000, and then open each folder in the Exploring window and select all items in each folder. Minimize the Exploring window and drag the items into the appropriate window in Outlook. For example, select all of the contents of the Contacts folder and drag them into the Contacts window in Outlook 2000. If you are teaching this course after July 2000, you should change the Due Dates on the sample tasks so that they do not display as overdue.

Notes on Using Exchange Server

Unlike Outlook 97, nearly all of the messaging features of Outlook 2000 are available to users on the Internet—as long as both the sending and receiving parties are using Outlook 2000 to send, open, and respond to Internet e-mail. This book focuses on using these Internet techniques, which are identical to the techniques for using Outlook on a corporate *intranet.*

However, you might wish to modify some Internet-based messaging exercises with an Exchange Server approach. Essentially, the steps are the same as with the Internet approach; however, students would use their Exchange Server

Postoffice names created by the Postoffice administrator and found in the Global Address List, rather than the Contacts list. To use this approach, you will need to arrange with the Exchange Server administrator for the network to have sufficient mailbox names for all members of each class.

Using the Lesson Content

The instructional components in each lesson of this book can be handled in different ways to match each instructor's teaching style and the different learning styles and background levels of each student. The following sections explain lesson components and suggest ways that each component can be used both in class and by students after class.

E-Mail Approach

To facilitate and demonstrate sending e-mail reliably during class, a few real, functioning e-mail addresses have been set up and are included in the exercises. To demonstrate receiving e-mail, each student sends a message to a class partner. For that reason, you should pair students into teams, and then have one student send e-mail to his or her partner (using e-mail addresses set up by you or your system administrator), and then have the partner respond to the other individual's e-mail.

Performance Objectives

Each lesson begins with clearly stated objectives, which set the expectations for the lesson and provide a sense of accomplishment as each objective is completed. The objectives also serve as a "mini" table of contents for each lesson. It is suggested that you briefly review the objectives with students at the start of each lesson.

Concepts

Concepts begin with a **For Your Information** heading, which is accompanied by an "open book" icon, as shown below:

For Your Information

The For Your Information paragraph provides a brief, general introduction to the concepts that follow.

The “open book” icon indicates that the following information is preparatory in nature, or can be read as reference information after class. The subheadings and text that follow the For Your Information paragraph contain information about each concept or task that will be demonstrated in the subsequent TRY IT exercise, and include generic procedures for performing each task, in a bulleted format with numbers as shown below:

To redisplay window items after a filter has been applied:

❶ Right-click a blank area of the window of the folder that is open.

❷ Click Filter.

❸ Click the Clear All button.

❹ Click OK.

It is not necessary to have students read through this conceptual material in class or to provide a thorough lecture for every concept and the accompanying bulleted numbered steps. Many instructors prefer to briefly review the concepts prior to the TRY ITS, and then direct students to the material so that they can refer to it for refresher purposes when they use the book on their own after class.

The generic, bulleted numbered steps in each concept can also be used to demonstrate more complex tasks prior to students performing a particular TRY IT exercise. For instance, if a projection screen is available in class, you can direct students to follow along with the bulleted numbered steps as you demonstrate a complex task on screen.

The bulleted numbered steps also have special value for after-class reference use. Many computer training books simply provide step-by-step examples similar to the TRY IT exercises in this book, without a general explanation of the associated tasks that are being carried out. However, when students return to their own computers at work or at home, they discover that the highly specific steps in the exercises do not relate directly to the real tasks they are trying to accomplish.

With this student need in mind, the bulleted numbered steps in the Concepts sections provide a way for students to work through the generic steps to complete a task on their own, translating each generic step into the specific step they need for the task at hand (such as replacing the generic instruction with their specific file or folder, or location within their own file).

TRY IT Exercises

These are the hands-on exercises that form the core of classroom instruction. ActiveEducation clearly differentiates the TRY IT Exercises from the general concept steps using several methods. First, each exercise begins with a heading similar to this one:

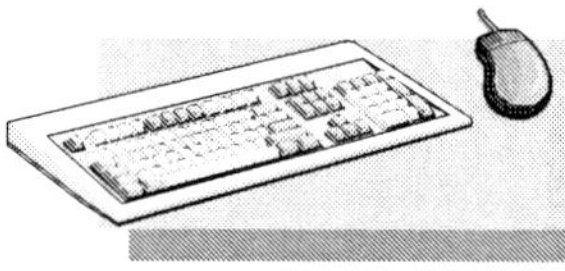

TRY IT 1–5 — SEARCH FOR E-MAIL MESSAGES

The keyboard and mouse icon in the heading indicates that the following steps are to be performed at the computer.

Each basic step in the TRY IT exercise is numbered. Substeps begin with a word or phrase in small caps, which also indicates to the student how the step will be performed (CLICK, DOUBLE-CLICK, RIGHT-CLICK, TYPE, PRESS). The words FIRST, THEN, and NEXT are also used for substeps that require a more general instruction.

The following conventions are used for substeps within the TRY IT exercises:

- When two keys are joined by a plus sign, press the first key, and while holding it down, press the second key.

  Example: **Ctrl+Home**

- Characters to type and keys to press are bolded.

  Examples:

  TYPE: **Thanks for the message.**

  PRESS: **Enter**

- Menu items and command buttons to click appear in bold.

  Examples: CLICK: **File** on the menu bar.

  CLICK: **OK**

  (Many instructions also include the button icon to be used.)

- Computer responses appear in a gray box, with top and bottom borders, like this:

  The contacts are assigned to the Picnic category.

Tips

Tips appear in the left margin of TRY IT exercises, and provide helpful hints, shortcuts, or alternative techniques. Tips look like this:

TIP

You can save any Advanced Find search as a file to use at a later time. Click **Save Search** on the File menu in the Advanced Find dialog box, and then save it as a file. To open a saved search, click **Open Search** on the File menu in the Advanced Find dialog box and open the saved search file.

Notes

Notes appear in both the concept sections of the book and the TRY IT exercises, and denote alternative approaches or additional information. Each note appears in a gray box and begins with a "push-pin note" icon, as shown below:

If the Permissions tab is not available, either you are not the owner of the folder, or you are not connected to the network.

QuickLook Summaries

QuickLook summaries are provided for additional reinforcement and retention of the major concepts and techniques learned in each lesson. Instructors frequently tell us that the Summaries are one of the most valuable components of ActiveEducation books, because they provide an "at a glance" review of the steps for all tasks performed during the lesson.

SkillCheck Exercises

Each lesson ends with a hands-on exercise that provides the students with a basic set of tasks to complete. The purpose of the exercise is to test and reinforce the skills and concepts learned in each lesson. For this reason, the steps in each SkillCheck are general in nature, and often require students to use judgment, creativity, and recall in completing the exercise. Students can perform the exercises either in class or independently after class as review/reinforcement.

MOUS OBJECTIVES

Core Skills

Objective	Activity	Course	Page
OL2000.1	**Use Outlook 2000 Mail To Communicate with Others Inside and Outside Your Company**		
OL2000.1.1	Read mail	Introduction	66
OL2000.1.2	Send mail	Introduction	50
OL2000.1.3	Compose mail by entering text	Introduction	50
OL2000.1.4	Print mail	Introduction	73
OL2000.1.5	Address mail by entering text	Introduction	50
OL2000.1.6	Use mail features (forward, reply, recall)	Introduction	62, 67
OL2000.1.7	Use address book to address mail	Introduction	111
OL2000.1.8	Flag mail messages	Intermediate	154
OL2000.1.9	Navigate within mail		
OL2000.1.10	Find messages	Intermediate	18
OL2000.1.11	Configure basic mail print options	Introduction	73
OL2000.1.12	Work with attachments	Introduction	54
OL2000.1.13	Add a signature to mail	Intermediate	89
OL2000.1.14	Customize the look of mail	Introduction	52
OL2000.1.15	Use mail templates to compose mail	Intermediate	112
OL2000.1.16	Integrate and use mail with other Outlook components	Intermediate	132
OL2000.1.17	Customize menu and task bars	Intermediate	7
OL2000.2	**Use Outlook 2000 To Manage Messages**		
OL2000.2.1	Create folders	Introduction	166
OL2000.2.2	Sort mail	Intermediate	74
OL2000.2.3	Set viewing options	Introduction	83
OL2000.2.4	Archive mail messages	Intermediate	81
OL2000.2.5	Filter a view	Intermediate	21
OL2000.3	**Use the Outlook 2000 Calendar**		
OL2000.3.1	Navigate within the Calendar	Introduction	121
OL2000.3.2	Schedule appointments and events	Introduction	131

Objective	Activity	Course	Page
OL2000.3.3	Set reminders	Introduction	132
OL2000.3.4	Print in Calendar	Introduction	128
OL2000.3.5	Schedule multi-day events	Intermediate	139
OL2000.3.6	Configure Calendar print options	Intermediate	126
OL2000.3.7	Customize the Calendar view	Introduction	122
OL2000.3.8	Schedule recurring appointments	Introduction	135
OL2000.3.9	Customize menu and task bars		
OL2000.3.10	Add and remove meeting attendees	Intermediate	133
OL2000.3.11	Plan meetings involving others	Intermediate	131
OL2000.3.12	Save a personal or team Calendar as a Web page	Intermediate	142
OL2000.3.13	Book office resources directly (e.g., conference rooms)	Intermediate	132
OL2000.3.14	Integrate Calendar with other Outlook components	Introduction	144, 153, 156
OL2000.4	**Navigate and Use Outlook 2000 Effectively**		
OL2000.4.1	Use Outlook Help and Office Assistant	Introduction	24, 49
OL2000.4.2	Move items between folders	Introduction	166
OL2000.4.3	Navigate between Outlook components	Introduction	30
OL2000.4.4	Modify the Outlook Master Categories List	Intermediate	13
OL2000.4.5	Assign items to a category	Intermediate	8
OL2000.4.6	Sort information using categories	Intermediate	16
OL2000.4.7	Use the Office Clipboard	Intermediate	113
OL2000.5	**Use Contacts**		
OL2000.5.1	Create, edit, and delete contacts	Introduction	99, 105
OL2000.5.2	Send contact information via e-mail	Intermediate	94
OL2000.5.3	Organize contacts by category	Introduction	108
OL2000.5.4	Manually record an activity in a journal	Intermediate	184
OL2000.5.5	Link activities to a Contact	Introduction	113
OL2000.5.6	Sort contacts using fields	Intermediate	157
OL2000.6	**Use Tasks**		
OL2000.6.1	Create and update one-time tasks	Introduction	153
OL2000.6.2	Accept and decline tasks	Intermediate	191
OL2000.6.3	Organize tasks using categories	Intermediate	8

Objective	Activity	Course	Page
OL2000.6.4	Assign tasks to others	Introduction	155
OL2000.6.5	Create tasks from other Outlook components	Introduction	176
OL2000.6.6	Change the view for tasks	Introduction	162
OL2000.7	**Integrate Office Applications and Other Applications with Outlook 2000 Components**		
OL2000.7.1	Create and use Office documents inside Outlook 2000	Introduction	190
OL2000.8	**Use Notes**		
OL2000.8.1	Create and edit notes	Introduction	175
OL2000.8.2	Organize and view notes	Introduction	176
OL2000.8.3	Customize notes	Introduction	178

Expert Skills

Objective	Activity	Course	Page
OL2000E.1	**Use Outlook 2000 Mail To Communicate with Others Inside and Outside Your Company**		
OL2000E.1.1	Work off-line or use remote mail	Intermediate	49
OL2000E.1.2	Add a vCard to a message	Intermediate	94
OL2000E.1.3	Create re-usable mail templates	Intermediate	112
OL2000E.1.4	Use mail with Office applications	Introduction	195
OL2000E.2	**Use Outlook 2000 to manage messages**		
OL2000E.2.1	Customize the look of mail	Introduction	52
OL2000E.2.2	Create a personal address book	Intermediate	97
OL2000E.2.3	Customize menu and task bars		
OL2000E.2.4	Track when mail messages are delivered or read	Intermediate	77
OL2000E.2.5	Create a personal distribution list	Intermediate	101
OL2000E.2.6	Create a Quick Synchronization group	Intermediate	51
OL2000E.2.7	Synchronize by message size	Intermediate	52
OL2000E.2.8	Organize mail using Rules Wizard	Intermediate	68

Objective	Activity	Course	Page
OL2000E.3	**Use the Outlook 2000 Calendar**		
OL2000E.3.1	Configure Calendar options	Introduction	122
OL2000E.3.2	Share Calendar information with other applications over the Internet	Intermediate	146
OL2000E.3.3	Schedule real-time meetings (NetMeeting)	Intermediate	134
OL2000E.3.4	Schedule times to watch broadcasts using NetShow	Intermediate	141
OL2000E.4	**Share Folders and Files with Other Outlook Users and with Users Inside and Outside of the Company**		
OL2000E.4.1	Use Netfolders and public folders	Intermediate	42
OL2000E.4.2	Grant delegate access	Intermediate	36
OL2000E.4.3	Grant permissions to folders	Intermediate	42
OL2000E.5	**Navigate and Use Outlook 2000 Effectively**		
OL2000E.5.1	Customize and use Outlook Today	Intermediate	4
OL2000E.5.2	Configure time zone information	Introduction	122
OL2000E.5.3	Manage favorite Web site addresses	Introduction	197
OL2000E.5.4	Import and export data between Outlook and other mail applications	Intermediate	56
OL2000E.5.5	Create Outlook forms	Intermediate	172
OL2000E.5.6	Create a shortcut to a file on your Outlook Bar	Introduction	26
OL2000E.6	**Use Contacts**		
OL2000E.6.1	Flag contacts for follow-up (reminder)	Intermediate	154
OL2000E.6.2	Customize Contacts menu and task bars	Intermediate	7

Objective	Activity	Course	Page
OL2000E.6.3	Integrate Contacts with other Outlook components	Introduction	111
OL2000E.6.4	Use Contacts with Office applications	Intermediate	162
OL2000E.7	**Use Tasks**		
OL2000E.7.1	Create and update recurring tasks	Intermediate	154
OL2000E.7.2	Customize menu and task bars	Intermediate	7
OL2000E.7.3	Record tasks for any Office file with the journal	Intermediate	184
OL2000E.7.4	Set delegate access to share tasks with two or more people	Intermediate	191
OL2000E.8	**Integrate Office Applications and Other Applications with Outlook 2000 Components**		
OL2000E.8.1	Import and export data between Outlook and other Office applications	Intermediate	107
OL2000E.8.2	Use Mail Merge with Word	Intermediate	162
OL2000E.9	**Use the Fax Service from within Outlook 2000**		
OL2000E.9.1	Receive a fax	Intermediate	204
OL2000E.9.2	Create and send a fax from within Outlook 2000	Intermediate	202
OL2000E.9.3	Customize a fax	Intermediate	203
OL2000E.10	**Use Newsreader**		
OL2000E.10.1	Send and receive information through Newsreader	Intermediate	60
OL2000E.10.2	Set up Newsreader	Intermediate	60

CONTENTS

Lesson 2: Using Files and Folders 29

Lesson 3: Modifying Mail 67

Scope of Course

This course discusses intermediate topics including customizing Outlook, categorizing items, searching for items, filtering items, sharing folders, setting permissions, working offline, importing and exporting files, managing and customizing mail messages, managing e-mail addresses, creating templates and forms, scheduling, creating a Web page, managing contacts, using mail merge to create mailing labels, and responding to tasks.

Course Requirements

This course, *Microsoft Outlook 2000 Intermediate*, is designed to build on the skills you acquired in *Introduction to Microsoft Outlook 2000*. This course requires that you have completed *Introduction to Microsoft Outlook 2000* or have a working knowledge of basic Outlook operations.

At Lakewood Mountain Resort

Throughout this book, you will be presented with on-the-job scenarios for a fictitious company called Lakewood Mountain Resort, a vacation hotel and convention center located in the Rocky Mountains of Colorado. Through these scenarios, you will discover how Microsoft Outlook can be used to improve productivity and to help solve business problems.

Course Objectives

By the end of this course, you will be able to:

- Customize Outlook
- Use categories to organize items
- Search and filter items
- Share folders
- Grant permissions and delegate access
- Use Net Folders
- Work offline
- Import and export data
- Manage mail messages
- Manage e-mail addresses
- Use templates
- Configure Calendar options
- Schedule events and meetings
- Use the Calendar on the Web
- Share the Calendar over the Internet
- Manage Contacts
- Use mail merge
- Create a form
- Use Tasks effectively

Performance Objectives

You will learn how to:

- Use and customize Outlook Today
- Use, customize, and sort by categories
- Search and filter e-mail messages

Using and Customizing Outlook Today

For Your Information

Outlook Today provides a summary of your appointments for the day and a list of your tasks to be completed, and tells you how many new e-mail messages you have. If you want, you can set this page to be the first page that opens when you start Outlook, and you can change the way Outlook Today appears.

Customizing Outlook Today

You can customize Outlook Today based on your preferences and what items you want to see. Although this view is called Outlook Today, your "day at a glance" can be changed to your "week at a glance" to show all your appointments and tasks for the week ahead.

Outlook Today automatically displays the number of unread e-mail messages in your Inbox, in your Drafts folder, and in your Outbox. If you like, you can display other folders in Outlook Today. You can also change the overall appearance of Outlook Today by changing its color and layout.

To customize Outlook Today:

1. On the Outlook bar, click Outlook Today.
2. Click Customize Outlook Today in the top-right corner of the Outlook Today window to display the Customize Outlook Today window, shown on the following page.

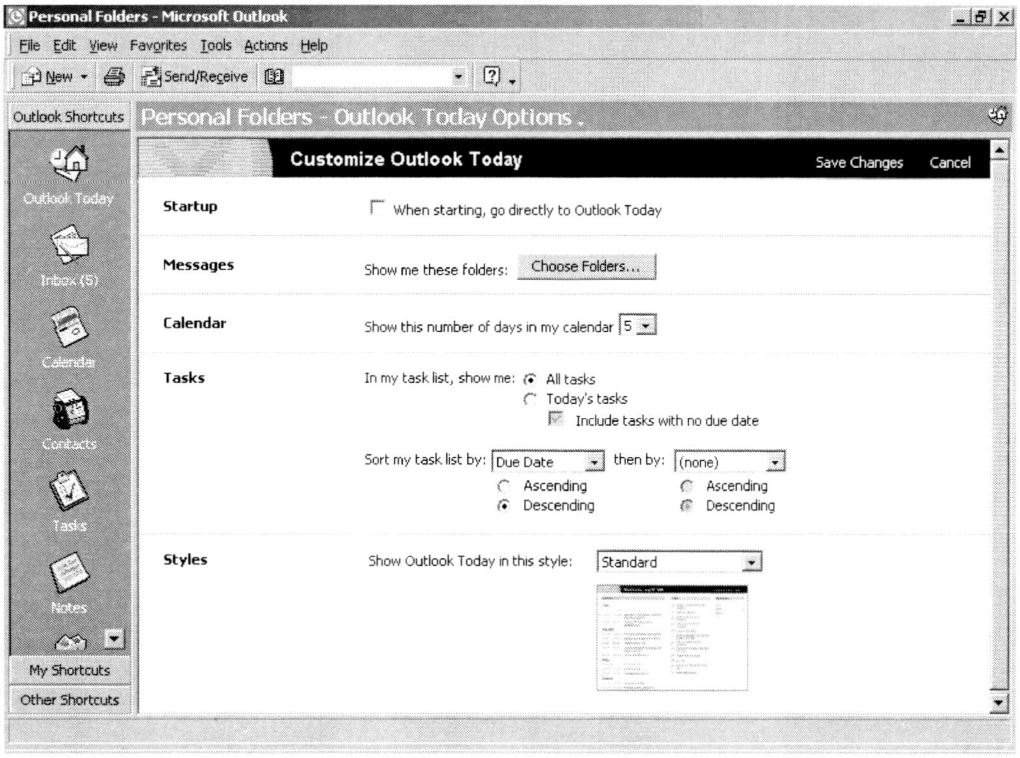

❸ In the Startup section, select the When starting, go directly to Outlook Today check box, if desired.

❹ In the Messages section, click the Choose Folders button to select the check boxes of the folders you want to appear in the Outlook Today window, and click OK.

❺ In the Calendar section, select how many days you want the calendar to display.

❻ In the Tasks section, select the desired options.

❼ In the Styles section, click an option in the Show Outlook Today in this style list.

❽ Click Save Changes in the top-right corner of the Customize Outlook Today window.

TRY IT 1–1 — CUSTOMIZE OUTLOOK TODAY

In this exercise, you will customize the look of Outlook Today.

1. **If necessary, start Outlook.**
2. **Open Outlook Today.**

   CLICK: The **Outlook Today**  icon on the Outlook bar.

   Outlook Today is displayed.

TIP

You can set Outlook to automatically display Outlook Today when you start Outlook by displaying the Customize Outlook Today window, clicking the **When starting, go directly to Outlook Today** check box, then clicking the **Save Changes** button.

3. **Customize Outlook Today.**

   CLICK: **Customize Outlook Today** in the top-right corner of the Outlook Today window.

   The Customize Outlook Today window is displayed.

   CLICK: The **Choose Folders** button in the Messages section.

   The Select Folder dialog box is displayed.

   THEN: Select the **Notes** and **Sent Items** check boxes.

   CLICK: **OK**

   The number of notes and sent items will be displayed in Outlook Today.

   CLICK: The drop-down arrow in the Calendar section and click **7**.

   Outlook Today will show your appointments for the next seven days.

CLICK: The drop-down arrow in the Styles section.

CLICK: **Winter**

A preview of the Winter style appears below the list box. Outlook Today will now be displayed in the colors and layout of the Winter style.

4. **Save the changes**.

CLICK: **Save Changes** in the top-right corner.

The customized Outlook Today page is displayed:

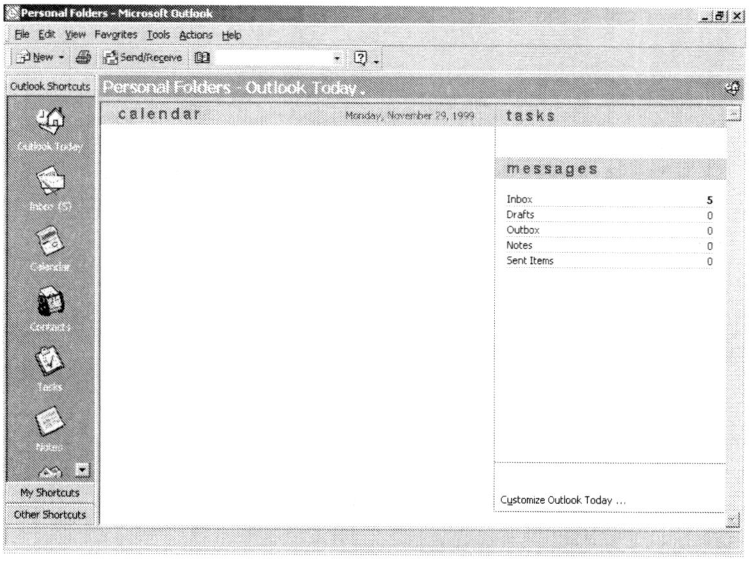

You can also modify Outlook menus and toolbars to better suit the way you work. To customize menus and toolbars, click Tools on the menu bar, and click Customize to display the Customize dialog box. This dialog box provides three tabs. Use the Toolbars tab to display other toolbars or even to create your own. Use the Commands tab to add buttons to toolbars and commands to menus by dragging items from the dialog box onto the desired toolbar or menu. For instance, you could add a button to the toolbar in Contacts to automatically address an e-mail message. (You could do this by assigning a hyperlink to the toolbar button. The hyperlink would link to the e-mail address.) Use the Options tab to change the way menus work (for example, to turn off personalized menus or to provide an animation effect when menus are displayed.

USING CATEGORIES

For Your Information

A *category* is a keyword or phrase that you can use to find, sort, filter, or group items. You can use categories to keep track of different types of items that are related but are stored in different folders. For example, the events coordinator at Lakewood Mountain Resort is planning a holiday party. To easily track all of her meetings, contacts, and e-mail messages concerning the holiday party, she has categorized these items under the Holiday category.

Using the Master Category List to Assign Items

Outlook supplies a list of categories you can assign items to, called the Master Category List. You can use this list as is or add your own categories to it. The following categories are available in the Master Category List.

- Business
- Competition
- Favorites
- Gifts
- Goals/Objectives
- Holiday
- Holiday Cards
- Hot Contacts
- Ideas
- International
- Key Customer
- Miscellaneous
- Personal
- Phone Calls
- Status
- Strategies
- Suppliers
- Time & Expenses
- VIP
- Waiting

Some of your items might relate to several categories and, in fact, you can assign an item to as many categories as needed. For example, the events coordinator at Lakewood Mountain Resort decided that some of her contacts for a holiday party might also be able to help her with an upcoming gag-gift exchange, so she also assigned those contacts to a category called Gifts.

To assign items to a category:

❶ Right-click the item(s) to assign to the category.

❷ Click Categories on the shortcut menu.

3. In the Available categories list, click the desired category or categories.
4. Click OK.

Viewing Items by Category

After you assign items to categories, you can then group items by the category you assigned them to. The steps for displaying the contents of the Inbox folder are slightly different than the steps for displaying the contents of the other folders.

To view the Inbox folder by categories:

1. Right-click a blank area of the window of the Inbox.
2. Click Customize Current View.
3. In the View Summary dialog box, click the Group By button.
4. Click the drop-down arrow in the Group items by section and click Categories.
5. Click OK twice.

To view all other folders by categories:

1. Click the folder you want to view by categories.
2. Click View on the menu bar.
3. Point to Current View on the View menu.
4. Click By Category.

Try It 1–2 — Assign an Item to a Category

In this exercise, you will assign items to categories in the Master Category List. You will also group items in your Inbox by category.

---

1. **Display the Inbox.**

2. **Assign an item to two categories.**

   RIGHT-
   CLICK: The e-mail message with the subject **Finance Review**.

   CLICK: **Categories** on the shortcut menu.

   The Categories dialog box is displayed:

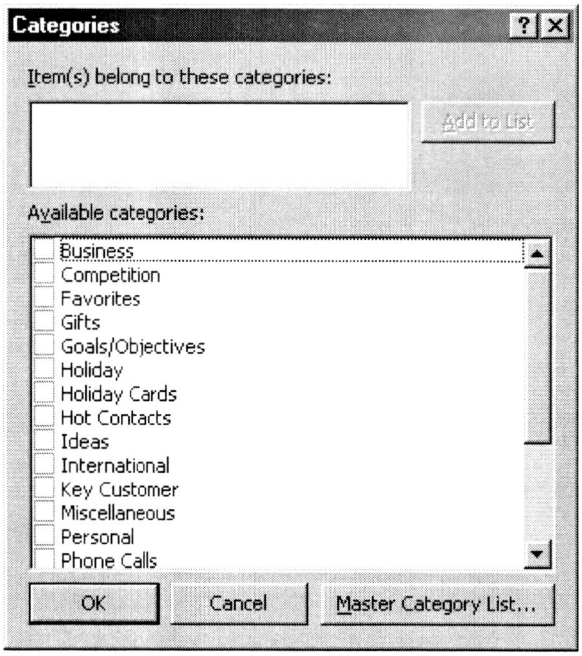

   THEN: In the Available categories list, select the **Business** and **Goals/Objectives** check boxes.

   CLICK: **OK**

   The e-mail message is assigned to both the Business and the Goals/Objectives categories.

3. **Assign multiple e-mail messages to a category.**

CLICK: The e-mail message with the subject *[Fwd: Eval for FSU]*.

PRESS & HOLD: **Ctrl** and click the e-mail message that contains the subject *League for Innovation.*

The e-mail messages are selected.

RIGHT-CLICK: Either of the selected messages.

CLICK: **Categories** on the shortcut menu.

THEN: In the Available categories list, select the **Goals/Objectives** check box.

CLICK: **OK**

The e-mail messages are assigned to the Goals/Objectives category.

4. **Display the Tasks folder.**

5. **Select a task in the Tasks folder.**

RIGHT-CLICK: The task with the subject **Call the Broadmoor for a quote.**

CLICK: **Categories** on the shortcut menu.

The Categories dialog box is displayed.

THEN: In the Available categories list, select the Business check box.

CLICK: **OK**

The task is assigned to the Business category.

6. **View the Tasks folder by category.**

CLICK: **View** on the menu bar.

THEN: Point to **Current View** on the View menu.

CLICK: **By Category**

The tasks are displayed by category.

CLICK: The **plus** [+] button to the left of the text *Categories: Business (1 item).*

The task that is assigned to this category is displayed.

7. **Restore the Tasks folder to its default view.**

CLICK: **View** on the menu bar.

THEN: Point to **Current View**.

CLICK: **Simple List**

8. **View the Inbox by category.**

FIRST: Display the Inbox.

RIGHT-CLICK: A blank area in the Message list.

CLICK: **Customize Current View** on the shortcut menu.

The View Summary dialog box appears, as shown in the figure below:

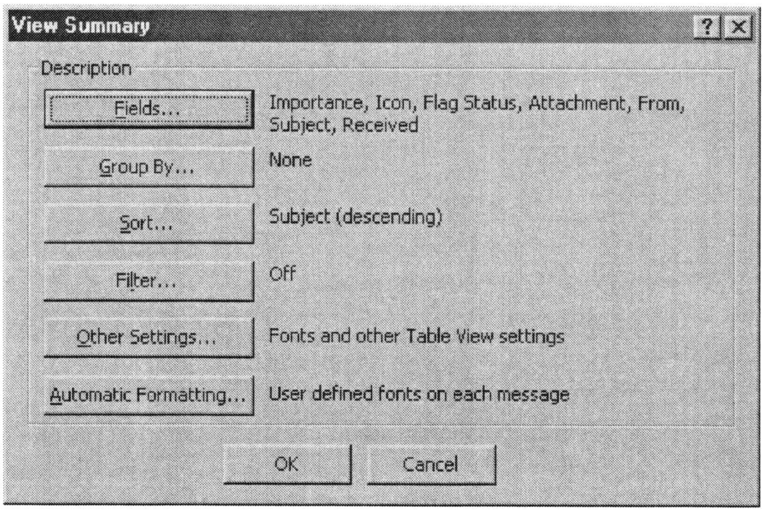

CLICK: The **Group By** button.

The Group By dialog box appears.

CLICK: The drop-down arrow in the Group items by section and click **Categories**.

TIP

You can display the messages in either ascending or descending order. In the Group By dialog box, click either the Ascending or Descending option in the Group items by section.

CLICK: **OK** twice.

The messages in your Inbox are grouped by category.

CLICK: The plus buttons to the left of the text *Categories: Business (1 item, 1 unread)* and *Categories: Goals/Objectives (3 items, 3 unread).*

The items in the categories are displayed. Notice that the Finance Review e-mail message is in both categories.

9. Restore the Inbox to its default view.

RIGHT-CLICK: A blank area in the message list.

CLICK: **Customize Current View** on the shortcut menu.

CLICK: The **Group By** button.

CLICK: The **Clear All** button.

CLICK: **OK** twice.

Modifying the Master Category List

If the Master Category List does not list a category that serves your needs, you can create your own category. The events coordinator at Lakewood Mountain Resort is organizing a company picnic. So she created a category called Picnic to track all items dealing with the picnic.

To add a new category to the Master Category List:

❶ Click Edit on the menu bar.

❷ Click Categories on the Edit menu.

❸ Click the Master Category List button to display the Master Category List dialog box, as shown below:

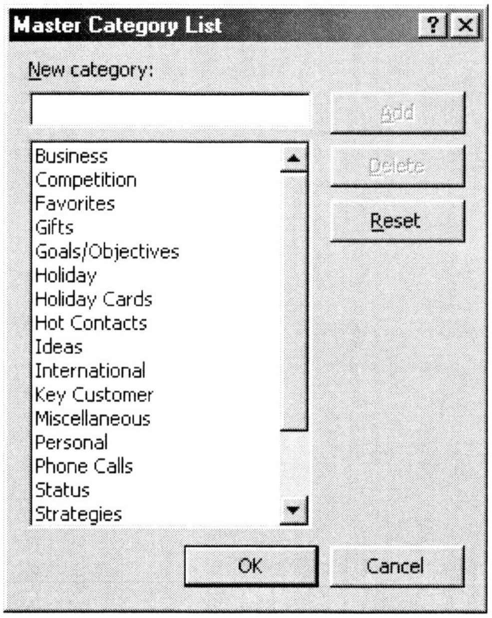

❹ In the New category text box, type a unique name for the category.

❺ Click the Add button.

❻ To create more categories, repeat steps 4 and 5.

❼ Click OK twice.

TRY IT 1–3 — MODIFY THE MASTER CATEGORY LIST

In this exercise, you will create and assign a new category to a contact.

---

1. **Display the Contacts folder.**
2. **Assign a contact to a new category.**

   CLICK: The contact **Christina Bauman**.

   PRESS & HOLD: **Ctrl** and click **John Chesbro** and **Ron Pronk**.

   The contacts are selected.

RIGHT-
CLICK: Any selected contact.

CLICK: **Categories** on the shortcut menu.

The Categories dialog box is displayed.

3. **Open the Master Category List.**

CLICK: The **Master Category List** button.

The Master Category List dialog box is displayed.

4. **Add a category to the Master Category List.**

TYPE: **Picnic** in the New category text box.

CLICK: The **Add** button.

TIP

If you want to return the Master Category List to the default categories, click the **Reset** button in the Master Category List dialog box. All categories you added will be deleted. These changes only affect the Master Category List. If you have items assigned to the deleted categories, they will keep their category assignments. You will have to manually delete or change the categories.

The category is added to the Master Category List.

CLICK: **OK**

THEN: Scroll down and click the Picnic check box.

CLICK: **OK**

The contacts are assigned to the Picnic category.

5. **Display the Contacts folder by category.**

CLICK: **View** on the menu bar.

THEN: Point to **Current View**.

CLICK: **By Category**

CLICK: The **plus** button to the left of the text *Categories: Picnic (3 items).*

The contacts assigned to the Picnic category are listed.

Sorting Information in Categories

You probably noticed that when you display an Outlook folder by category, the window is displayed in a table (row and column) format. The row under the folder name displays column headings (as shown below). If you position the mouse pointer over a column heading, a ScreenTip will appear that displays the text *Sort by: [name of column]*, for example *Sort by: Full Name*. Clicking the column heading will result in displaying the items in either ascending or descending order. Sorting categories allows you to quickly find specific e-mail messages, tasks, or contacts.

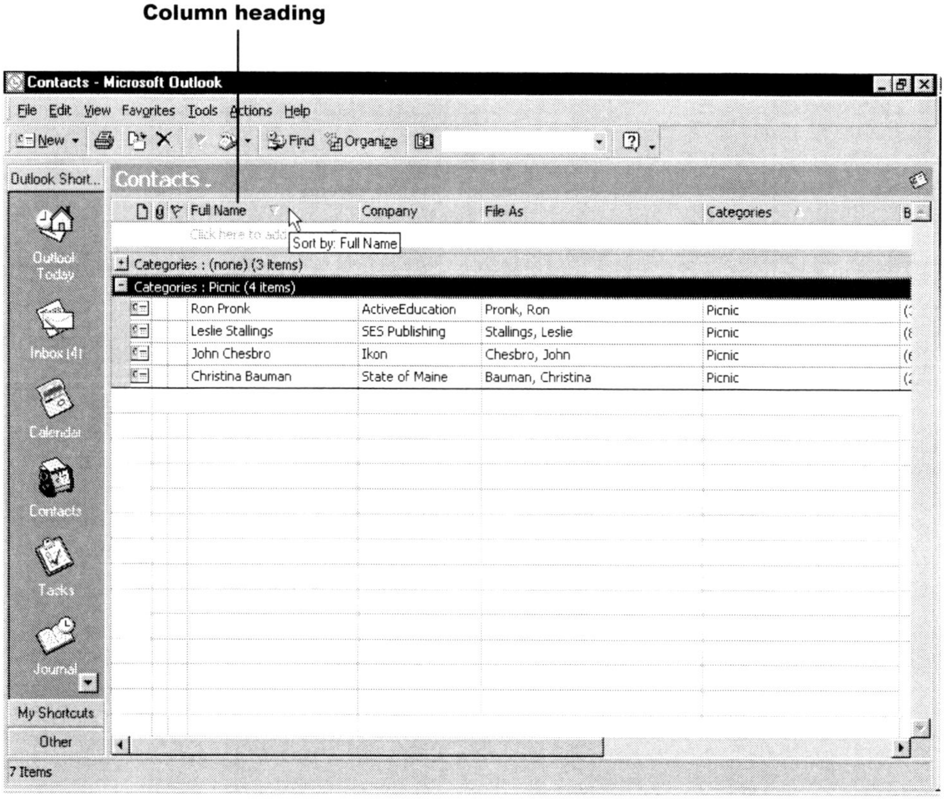

To sort information in categories:

- Click the column heading that you want to sort by to toggle between ascending and descending order.

TRY IT 1–4 — SORT INFORMATION IN CATEGORIES

In this exercise, you will sort the contacts in the Picnic category by full name, company, and how they are filed.

TIP

If you are not displaying the items in a folder by category, you can change the sort order by clicking **View** on the menu bar, pointing to **Current View**, and then clicking **Customize Current View**. Click the **Sort** button in the View Summary dialog box. Click the drop-down arrow in the "Sort items by" section, and click a field to sort by. Click the **Ascending** or **Descending** option for the sort order. To sort by an additional field, click a field in the "Then by" list. Click **OK** twice.

1. **Sort by Full Name.**

   CLICK: The Full Name column heading.

   The contacts are sorted by their first name in ascending order. An up arrow appears on the Full Name column heading.

   CLICK: The Full Name column heading again.

   The contacts are sorted by their first name in descending order. A down arrow appears on the Full Name column heading.

2. **Sort by Company.**

   CLICK: The Company column heading.

   The contacts are sorted by their company's name in ascending order. An up arrow appears on the Company column heading.

3. **Sort by File As.**

   CLICK: The File As column heading.

   The contacts are sorted by their last name in ascending order. An up arrow appears on the File As column heading.

4. **Restore the Contacts folder to its default view.**

   CLICK: **View** on the menu bar.

   THEN: Point to **Current View** on the View menu.

   CLICK: **Address Cards**

   The contacts are now displayed in Address Cards view.

SEARCHING AND FILTERING ITEMS

For Your Information

Outlook provides two different ways to locate items: searching and filtering. While the two methods can produce the same results, they are very different.

Using Find and Advanced Find

You use the Find feature and the Advanced Find dialog box to perform searches. The Find feature appears in a separate window pane and provides basic search capabilities for finding items in one folder. The results are displayed in the folder you searched in.

The Advanced Find dialog box allows you search using more specific criteria, such as finding items in every folder instead of in just one folder. If you click any item after the search results appear, the item will be displayed in the folder in which it was created.

The marketing director at Lakewood Mountain Resort needed to search for every item concerning her staff meetings. So she used the Advanced Find dialog box to search for these items in all of her folders.

To search for an item using the Find pane:

❶ Display the folder in which you want to search for an item.

❷ Click the Find button on the toolbar.

❸ In the Look for text box, type any text you want to search for in the folder, as shown in the figure below:

❹ Click the Find Now button.

To search for items using Advanced Find:

❶ Click Tools on the menu bar, and click Advanced Find on the Tools menu.

Or

Click Advanced Find in the Find pane.

❷ In the Advanced Find dialog box, select the criteria to base the search on in the various fields. (The options vary depending on the type of items you want to search for and in which folders you want to search.)

❸ Click the Find Now button.

Items that match the criteria you specified appear in the bottom of the Advanced Find dialog box, as shown below:

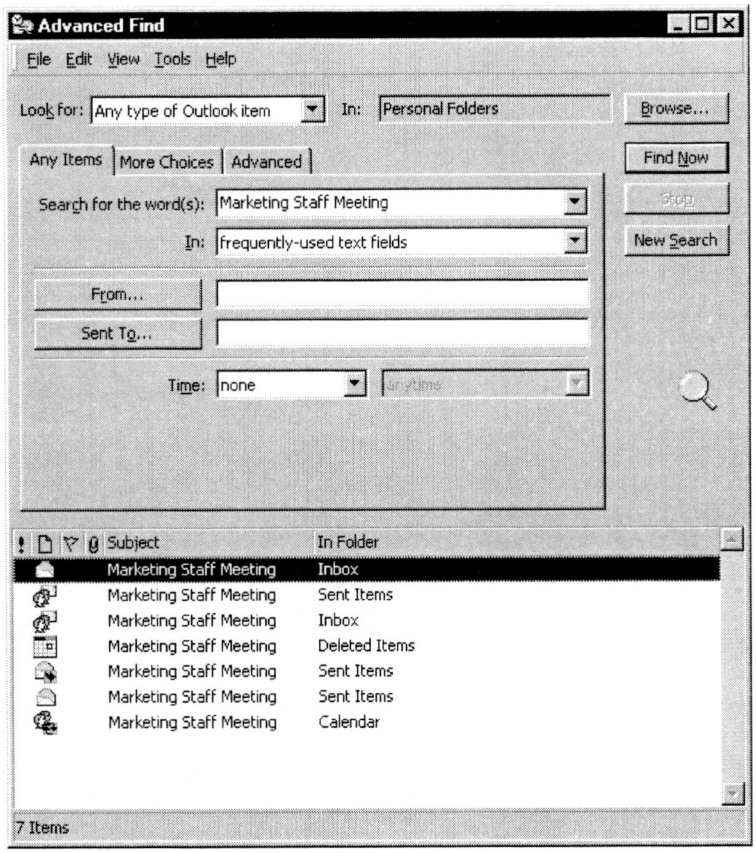

❹ Double-click the item that you want to view.

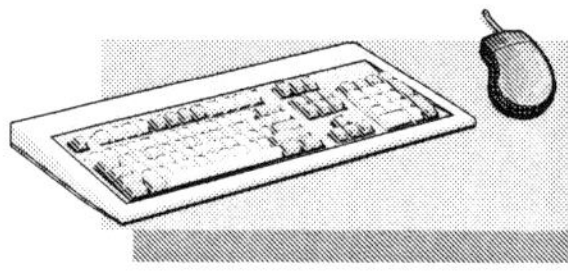

TRY IT 1–5 — SEARCH FOR E-MAIL MESSAGES

In this exercise, you will use Find and Advanced Find to perform searches.

---

1. **Display the Contacts folder, if necessary.**

2. **Open Find.**

   CLICK: The **Find** [Find] button on the toolbar.

   The Find pane appears.

   TYPE: **ASR** in the Look for text box.

   CLICK: The **Find Now** button.

   The contact that contains the text *ASR* is displayed.

3. **Perform a search using the Advanced Find dialog box.**

   CLICK: **Advanced Find** in the top-right corner of the Find pane.

   The Advanced Find dialog box appears.

   CLICK: The Look for drop-down arrow.

   THEN: Scroll up and click **Any type of Outlook item**.

   TYPE: **Web** in the Search for the word(s) text box.

   CLICK: The In drop-down arrow.

   CLICK: **frequently-used text fields**

   CLICK: The **More Choices** tab.

   CLICK: The **Categories** button.

   The Categories dialog box appears.

   CLICK: **Goals/Objectives**

   CLICK: **OK**

TIP

You can save any Advanced Find search as a file to use at a later time. Click **Save Search** on the File menu in the Advanced Find dialog box, and then save it as a file. To open a saved search, click **Open Search** on the File menu in the Advanced Find dialog box and open the saved search file.

4. **Run Advanced Find.**

   CLICK: The **Find Now** button.

   The Advanced Find dialog box displays a message from the Goals/Objectives category that has something to do with the word *Web*.

5. **Open a message.**

   DOUBLE-CLICK: The message displayed at the bottom of the dialog box.

   The message from the Goals/Objective category is displayed. The word *Web* is present in the body of the e-mail message.

   CLICK: The **Close** [X] button in the top-right corner of the message window.

6. **Restore all messages.**

   CLICK: The **Close** [X] button in the top-right corner of the Advanced Find dialog box.

   CLICK: The **Close** [X] button in the top-right corner of the Find pane.

   All of the contacts are redisplayed.

Showing or Hiding Items or Files Using a Filter

Using a filter is similar to performing a search—in fact, the Find and Filter dialog boxes are almost identical. However, there is one important difference. When you filter items, only those items that match your search criteria appear in the folder until you turn off the filter.

The marketing director applied a filter to her Inbox to display only those e-mail messages that were about her staff meetings. Although other e-mail messages were still in her Inbox, they were not displayed in the window. To redisplay all of her e-mail messages, she cleared the filter from the Inbox.

Filtering is extremely useful when you want to print only one or a few items, such as a single contact or two related tasks.

To apply a filter:

1. Right-click a blank area of the window of the folder that is displayed.

2. Click Filter on the shortcut menu to display the Filter dialog box, as shown in the following figure:

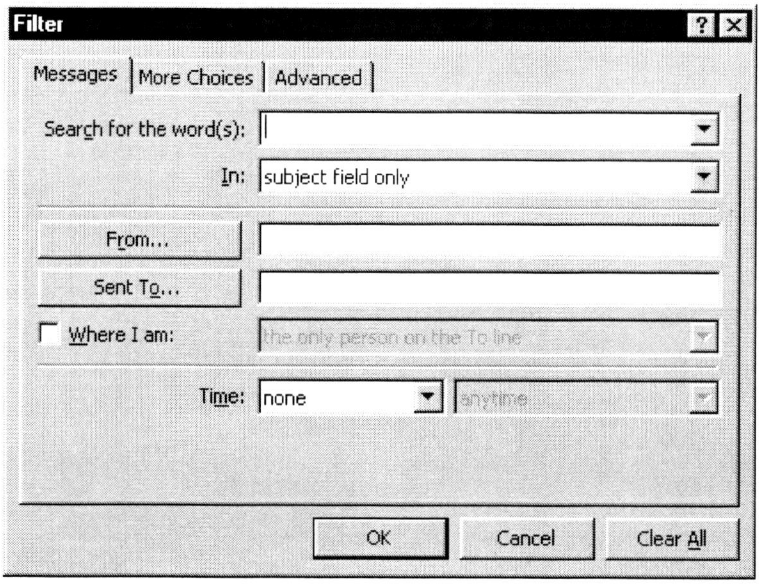

> If you are in the Journal folder or the Calendar folder, you must right-click a blank area of the window, click Customize Current View, and click the Filter button to display the Filter dialog box.

3. Select the filter options you want. To filter using additional criteria, such as a category or importance level, click the More Choices tab, and then select the options you want. To filter using additional or custom fields, click the Advanced tab, and then select the options you want.

> If you select more than one option, only the items that meet all of the criteria appear. However, if you type more than one search criteria in a field, Outlook will find items that contain one search word—not both. (For example, if you type *Web; credit*, Outlook might find one item that contains the word *Web*, and another item that contains the word *credit*. The items listed would not need to contain both search words.)

4. Click OK.

To redisplay window items after a filter has been applied:

❶ Right-click a blank area of the window of the folder that is open.

❷ Click Filter.

❸ Click the Clear All button.

❹ Click OK.

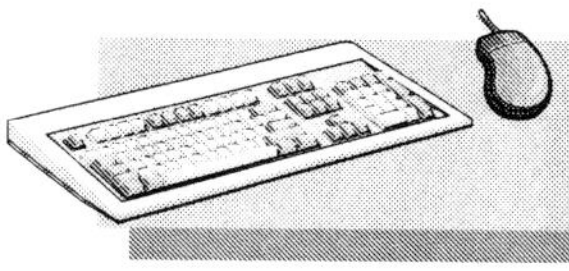

TRY IT 1–6 — USE A FILTER

In this exercise, you will apply a filter to view certain e-mail messages.

---

1. **Display the Inbox.**

2. **Open the Filter dialog box.**

   RIGHT-CLICK: A blank area of the message list.

   CLICK: **Filter** on the shortcut menu.

   The Filter dialog box is displayed.

3. **Set the filter options.**

   TYPE: **SES** in the Search for the words text box.

   CLICK: The In drop-down arrow.

   CLICK: **Subject field and message body**

   CLICK: The **More Choices** tab.

   THEN: Select the Match case check box.

   Selecting the Match case check box will display e-mail messages that have the text SES in all uppercase letters. Otherwise, e-mail messages that have words like "session" or "theses" will also be displayed.

CLICK: **OK**

The e-mail message containing the text SES is displayed in the Inbox. The words "Filter Applied" appear in the top-right corner of the Inbox window to remind you that you have other messages.

4. **Redisplay all e-mail messages in the Inbox.**

RIGHT-
CLICK: A blank area of the Message list.

CLICK: **Filter** on the shortcut menu.

The Filter dialog box is displayed.

CLICK: The **Clear All** button in the Filter dialog box.

CLICK: **OK**

QuickLook at Lesson 1

To	Do This
Customize Outlook Today	1. On the Outlook bar, click **Outlook Today**. 2. Click **Customize Outlook Today** in the top-right corner of the Outlook Today window. 3. In the Startup section, select the When starting, go directly to Outlook Today check box, if desired. 4. In the Messages section, click the **Choose Folders** button to select the check boxes of the folders you want to appear in the Outlook Today window, and click **OK**. 5. In the Calendar section, select how many days you want the calendar to display. 6. In the Tasks section, select the desired options. 7. In the Styles section, click an option in the Show Outlook Today in this style list. 8. Click the **Save Changes** button in the top-right corner of the Customize Outlook Today window.
Assign items to a category	1. Right-click the item(s) to assign the category. 2. Click **Categories** on the shortcut menu. 3. In the Available categories list, click the desired category or categories. 4. Click **OK**.
View the Inbox folder by categories	1. Right-click a blank area of the window of the inbox. 2. Click **Customize Current View**. 3. In the View Summary dialog box, click the **Group By** button. 4. Click the drop-down arrow in the Group items by section, and click Categories. 5. Click **OK** twice.
View all other folders by categories	1. Click the folder you want to view by categories. 2. Click **View** on the menu bar. 3. Point to **Current View** on the View menu. 4. Click **By Category**.

To	Do This
Add a new category to the Master Category List	**1.** Click **Edit** on the menu bar. **2.** Click **Categories** on the Edit menu. **3.** Click the **Master Category List** button to display the Master Category List dialog box. **4.** In the New category text box, type a unique name for the category. **5.** Click the **Add** button. **6.** To create more categories, repeat steps 4 and 5. **7.** Click **OK** twice.
Sort information in categories	**1.** Click the column heading that you want to sort by to toggle between ascending and descending order.
Search for an item using the Find pane	**1.** Display the folder in which you want to search for an item. **2.** Click the **Find** button on the toolbar. **3.** In the Look for text box, type any text you want to search for in the folder. **4.** Click the **Find Now** button.
Search for items using Advanced Find	**1.** Click **Tools** on the menu bar, and click **Advanced Find** on the Tools menu. *Or* Click **Advanced Find** in the Find pane. **2.** In the Advanced Find dialog box, select the criteria to base the search on in the various fields. (The options vary depending on the type of items you want to search for and in which folders you want to search.) **3.** Click the **Find Now** button. **4.** Double-click the item that you want to view.
Apply a filter	**1.** Right-click a blank area of the window of the folder that is displayed. **2.** Click **Filter** on the Shortcut menu to display the Filter dialog box. **3.** Select the filter options you want. To filter using additional criteria such as a category or importance level, click the **More Choices** tab, and then select the options you want. To filter using additional or custom fields, click the **Advanced** tab, and then select the options you want. **4.** Click **OK**.

To	Do This
Redisplay window items after a filter has been applied	**1.** Right-click a blank area of the window of the folder that is open. **2.** Click **Filter**. **3.** Click the **Clear All** button. **4.** Click **OK**.

SkillCheck – Lesson 1

1. Display Outlook Today.
2. Change the style of Outlook Today to the Summer style.
3. Add a category called Company Parties to the Master Category List.
4. Assign the contact Ron Pronk the new category.
5. Display the Inbox and sort the column heading From in descending order.
6. Use Advanced Find to search for e-mail messages about training.
7. Filter the Inbox to display only e-mail messages involving credit cards, then remove the filter.

Answers to the SkillChecks can be found here: **http://www.activeed.com/skanswers/outlook2.htm**

Performance Objectives

You will learn how to:

- Share a file folder with others
- Use Net Folders
- Work offline
- Import and export data

SHARING A FOLDER WITH OTHERS

For Your Information

If you work on a network, using Microsoft Exchange Server, you can share Outlook items with others by putting the items in a *public folder*. A public folder can contain messages or information that can be shared with designated users. The human resources manager at Lakewood Mountain Resort likes to have access to the calendars of all the managers so that she can see when a particular manager will be available to interview applicants.

Sharing Folders

When you share an Outlook folder, any user on the network that has permission can make changes to it, and all other users will see those changes. For example, if you share a task list with others, when someone completes a task, they can mark it as completed so that everyone involved can see that the task no longer has to be performed.

To create a shared folder:

❶ From any private folder, click File on the menu bar.

❷ Point to New on the File menu, then click Folder to display the Create New Folder dialog box, as shown below:

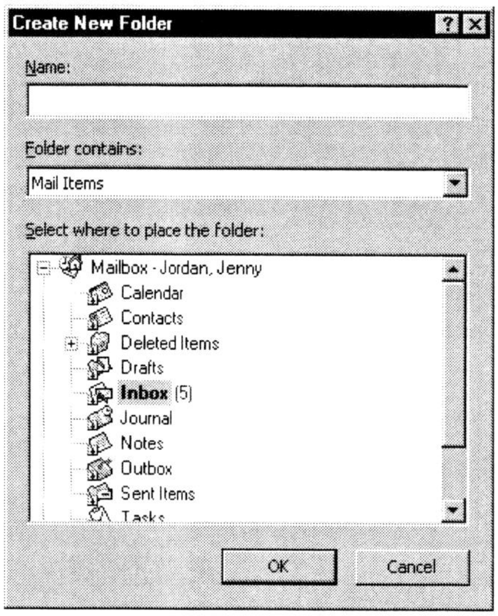

❸ In the Name box, type a name.

❹ Click the Folder Contains drop-down arrow, and then click the type of item the folder will contain.

❺ In the Select where to place the folder box, click the plus sign to the left of Public Folders, then click All Public Folders.

❻ Click OK.

❼ Click Yes or No in the alert box that appears.

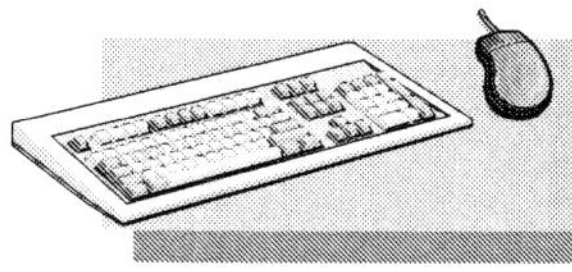

TRY IT 2–1 — SHARE A PRIVATE FOLDER WITH OTHERS

In this exercise, you will create a Tasks folder and share it with others.

---

1. Create a folder to share.

CLICK: **File** on the menu bar.

THEN: Point to **New** on the File menu.

CLICK: **Folder**

The Create New Folder dialog box appears.

TYPE: [Your first and last name]**'s Company Party Tasks**

CLICK: The Folder contains drop-down arrow and click **Task Items**.

THEN: In the Select where to place the folder list, click the plus sign to the left of Public Folders, and click **All Public Folders**.

CLICK: **OK**

An alert box appears, asking if you want to add a shortcut to this new tasks folder to your Outlook bar.

CLICK: **No**

2. Display the Folder List.

TIP

If you choose to display the Folder List by clicking the folder name in the Folder banner, you must click the **push pin** icon  so that you can right-click items.

3. **Create tasks.**

FIRST: Navigate to All Public Folders.

THEN: Scroll, if necessary, and click your Company Party Tasks folder.

The Tasks folder is opened.

CLICK: In the Click here to add a new Task text box.

TYPE: **Order invitations.**

PRESS: **Enter**

TYPE: **Book a band.**

PRESS: **Enter**

TYPE: **Call caterer.**

PRESS: **Enter**

The tasks are created.

4. **Mark a task as completed.**

CLICK: The check box to the left of *Book a band.*

The task is marked as completed. If someone else on the network opens this folder, he or she will see that this task is completed.

5. **Mark a task in your partner's public folder as completed.**

FIRST: Navigate to All Public Folders in the Folder List.

CLICK: Your class partner's Company Party Tasks folder.

Notice that *Book a band* is already marked as completed, because your partner, like you, marked it as completed in the previous step.

CLICK: The check box to the left of *Order invitations.*

An alert box appears, stating that you don't have permission to modify the items in this folder. You will learn how to set permissions in the next exercise.

CLICK: **OK**

Granting Permission to Folders

Before users on the network can access a public folder you created, you must grant each person permission to use the folder.

When you grant permission to a network user, you can specify how much involvement you want the user to have. These levels of involvement are called *roles*. Outlook has nine different roles you can assign a user to:

Role Type	Options Available
Owner	All
Publishing Editor	Create, read, edit, and delete items in folder, and create subfolders
Editor	Create, read, edit, and delete items in folder
Publishing Author	Create and read items in folder, create subfolders, and edit and delete items that he or she created
Author	Create and read items in folder, and edit and delete items that he or she created
Nonediting Author	Create and read items in folder
Reviewer	Read items only
Contributor	Create items only; contents of the folder do not appear
None	None

To grant permissions to folders:

❶ Display the Folder List.

❷ Right-click the folder.

❸ Click Properties on the shortcut menu.

❹ Click the Permissions tab on the Properties dialog box, as shown below:

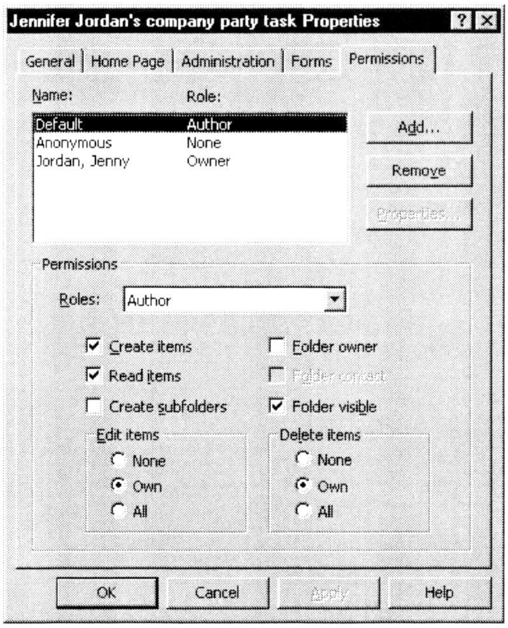

If the Permissions tab is not available, either you are not the owner of the folder, or you are not connected to the network.

❺ Click the Add button to display the Add Users dialog box, as shown below:

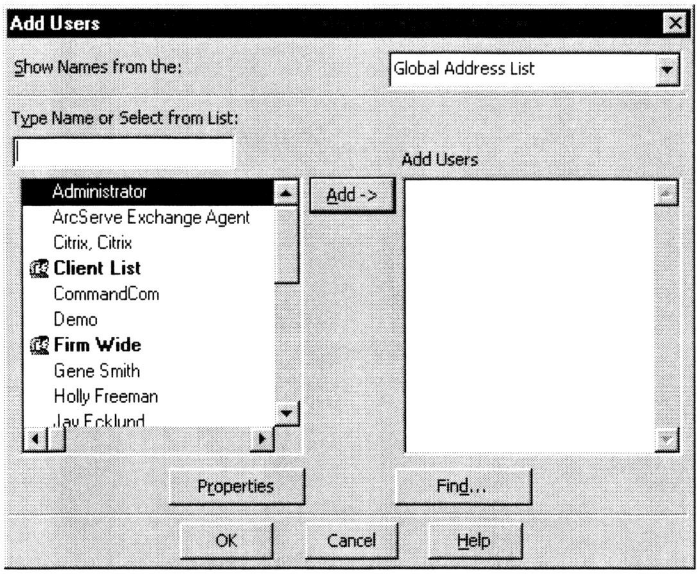

❻ Type or click the name of the person to be added to the permissions list.

❼ Click the Add button.

❽ Click OK.

❾ Select the name in the Name list.

❿ Click the Roles drop-down arrow, and click a role to determine the level of permission for the user.

⓫ Click OK.

TRY IT 2–2 — GRANT PERMISSIONS

In this exercise, you will grant a contact permission to your Company Party Tasks folder.

---

1. **Display the Folder List.**

2. **Grant permission to the Company Party Tasks folder.**

RIGHT-CLICK: The Company Party Tasks folder.

> A shortcut menu appears.

CLICK: **Properties** on the shortcut menu.

> The Properties dialog box appears.

CLICK: The **Permissions** tab on the Properties dialog box.

CLICK: The **Add** button.

THEN: Scroll if necessary, and click your class partner's name.

CLICK: The **Add** button.

CLICK: **OK**

CLICK: Your class partner's name in the Name list.

> Notice that the role Author has automatically been assigned to your class partner.

CLICK: The Roles drop-down arrow, and click **Publishing Editor**.

Your class partner will be able to create, read, edit, and delete items in the folder and create subfolders.

CLICK: **OK**

TIP

You can set permissions to a folder to as many users as desired.

The permissions are set.

3. **Modify your class partner's Company Party Tasks folder.**

   FIRST: In the Folder List, click your partner's Company Party Tasks folder.

   NEXT: Select the check box to the left of the Order invitations task.

   Outlook allows you to mark the task as complete.

   DOUBLE-CLICK: The Call caterer task.

   CLICK: The Due Date drop-down arrow, and click tomorrow's date.

   CLICK: The **Save and Close** button.

   The Due Date appears in the task list.

4. **View your Company Party Tasks folder.**

   Notice that the tasks in your folder have been updated by your class partner.

Granting Delegate Access

You can appoint or delegate someone to send or maintain items on your behalf. For example, the marketing director at Lakewood Mountain Resort is going on vacation so she has granted *delegate access* to her assistant for the Inbox and Calendar folders. Her assistant will be able to access these folders while she's gone.

As with granting permissions, you can also specify what role you want the delegate to have. The role types used for granting permissions are listed in the table on the following page.

Role Type	Options Available
None	None
Reviewer	Can read items
Author	Can read and create items
Editor	Can read, create, and modify items

To grant delegate access:

❶ Click Tools on the menu bar.

❷ Click Options on the Tools menu.

❸ Click the Delegates tab, as shown below:

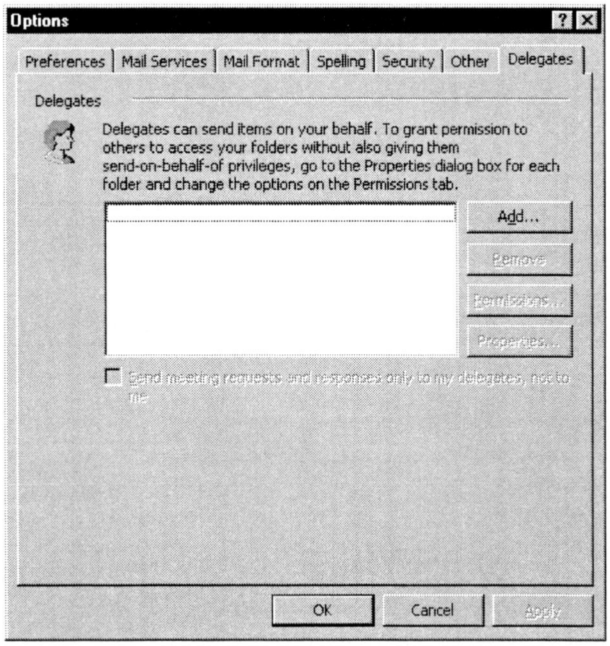

❹ Click the Add button.

❺ Type or click the name of the delegate.

❻ Click the Add button.

❼ Click OK.

❽ Select the appropriate permissions for the desired folders.

❾ Click OK twice.

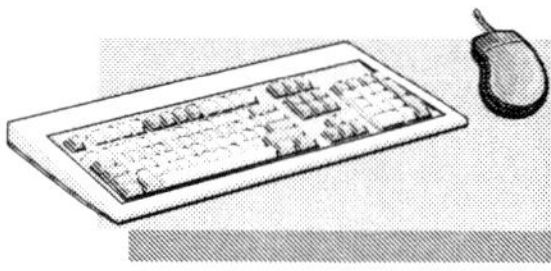

TRY IT 2–3 — GRANT DELEGATE ACCESS

In this exercise, you will grant your class partner delegate access to the Tasks and Inbox folders.

TIP

You can delete a delegate's access by clicking the delegate's name in the Delegates list on the Delegates tab, then clicking the **Remove** button.

---

1. **Grant delegate access.**

   CLICK: **Tools** on the menu bar.

   CLICK: **Options** on the Tools menu.

   The Options dialog box appears.

   CLICK: The **Delegates** tab.

   CLICK: The **Add** button.

   The Add Users dialog box appears.

   CLICK: Your class partner's name.

   CLICK: The **Add** button.

   Your class partner is now a delegate.

2. **Set a delegate's permissions.**

   CLICK: **OK**

   The Delegate Permissions dialog box appears, as shown on the following page.

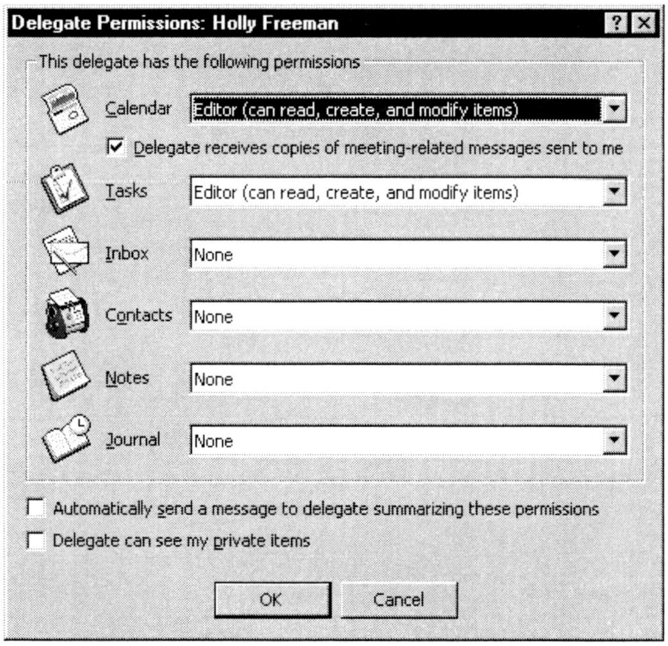

CLICK: The Calendar drop-down arrow.

CLICK: **None**

Your class partner will not have access to your Calendar.

TIP

You can grant delegate access to more than one user at a time. In the Add Users dialog box, click a contact, click the **Add** button, click another contact, and click the **Add** button again. Repeat as necessary to add all of the desired contacts. Click **OK**, and set permissions for the desired folders.

CLICK: The Tasks drop-down arrow, and click **Author**.

Your partner will be able to read and create items in the Tasks folder.

CLICK: The Inbox drop-down arrow, and click **Reviewer**.

Your partner will only be able to read e-mail messages in the Inbox folder.

CLICK: **OK** twice.

The delegate's permissions are set.

A delegate can access another user's folders by clicking File on the menu bar, pointing to Open, and clicking Other User's Folder. Type the name of the other user, click the Folder drop-down arrow, click the folder that you have access to, and click OK.

3. **Test delegate access privileges.**

CLICK: **File** on the menu bar.

THEN: Point to **Open**.

CLICK: **Other User's Folder**

The Open Other User's Folder dialog box appears, as shown below:

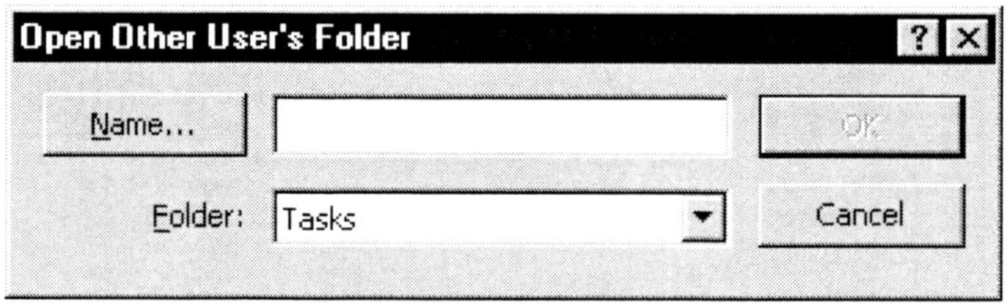

NEXT: In the Name text box, type your class partner's name.

CLICK: The Folder drop-down arrow, and click **Inbox**.

CLICK: **OK**

Your class partner's Inbox appears in its own window. Since you only have Reviewer access, you can only read the e-mail messages in the Inbox.

CLICK: The **Close** button in the top-right corner of your partner's Inbox window.

Your partner's Inbox is closed.

Using Net Folders

For Your Information

Suppose you want to give someone outside your network access to one of your Outlook folders. For example, the marketing assistant at Lakewood Mountain Resort wanted to give a friend access to her Calendar folder so her friend would know what days she was available for lunch. Outlook provides a way for you to share certain folders with anyone over the Internet. You can do this by using *Net Folders*. Simply designate a folder that you want to share and send "subscriptions" to others so that they can access this folder. If the subscriber accepts the subscription, the folder will be copied to the subscriber's computer. If you make any changes to the folder, the items will be updated for all of the subscribers.

Publishing a Net Folder

To *publish* a Net Folder means to share a folder with specified people over the Internet. You can share a folder that you created and added items to, or you can share Outlook folders (except the Inbox, Outbox, or Exchange folders). You can share contacts, tasks, journals, notes, or calendars. If you want to share contacts or Calendar items with a subscriber, the subscriber must also use Outlook because these items are not usable by other e-mail programs.

After you publish a Net Folder, a message is automatically sent to the potential subscriber(s). To become a subscriber, he or she must click Accept in the message. However, recipients who do not use Outlook will only receive a notification message that they are subscribed.

Setting Subscriber Permissions to Net Folders

When you publish a Net Folder, you set subscriber permissions. The subscriber permissions are a lot like the permissions you set for the Public folders on Exchange Server. The table below details each type of permission:

Permission	Options Available
Reviewer	Read items and files, but cannot create, edit, or delete items or files
Contributor	Create and read items and files, but cannot edit or delete items or files
Author	Create and read items and files in folder, and edit and delete items that he or she created
Editor	Create, read, edit, and delete items and files in folder
Minimum	Receive items as attachments to e-mail messages; changes made are not updated in other members' folders (designated for users who do not use Outlook)

To publish a Net Folder and set permissions:

❶ Display the Folder List.

❷ If desired, create a folder that you want to share in the Personal Folders file.

Or

Copy an existing folder to your Personal Folders file.

❸ Click the folder that you want to share.

❹ Click File on the menu bar.

❺ Point to Share on the File menu.

❻ Click This Folder.

The Net Folder Wizard appears, as shown on the following page.

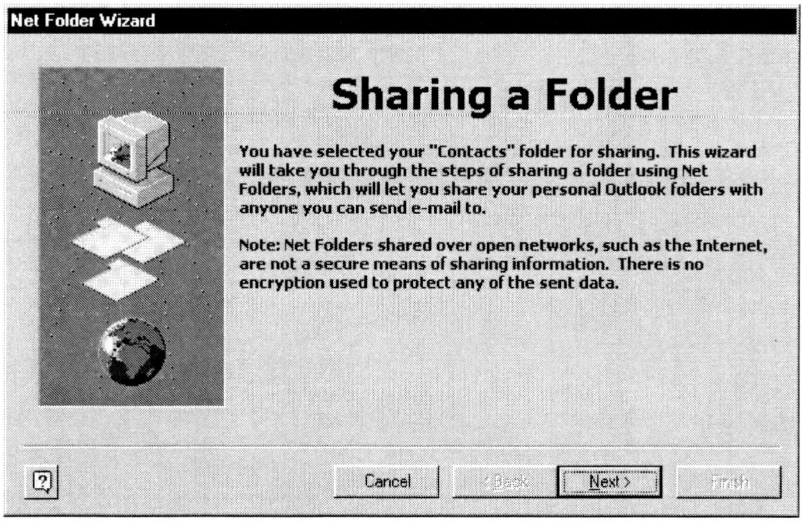

❼ If desired, close the Office Assistant.

❽ Click Next.

❾ Click the Add button.

❿ Click the Show Names from the drop-down arrow and click Contacts.

⓫ Type the name of the potential subscriber in the Type Name or Select from List text box.

Or

Select the name from the list.

⓬ Click the To button.

⓭ Click OK.

⓮ Click a name in the Member List box, if necessary.

⓯ Click the Permissions button and assign a level of permission to the potential subscriber in the Net Folder Sharing Permissions dialog box, as shown on the next page.

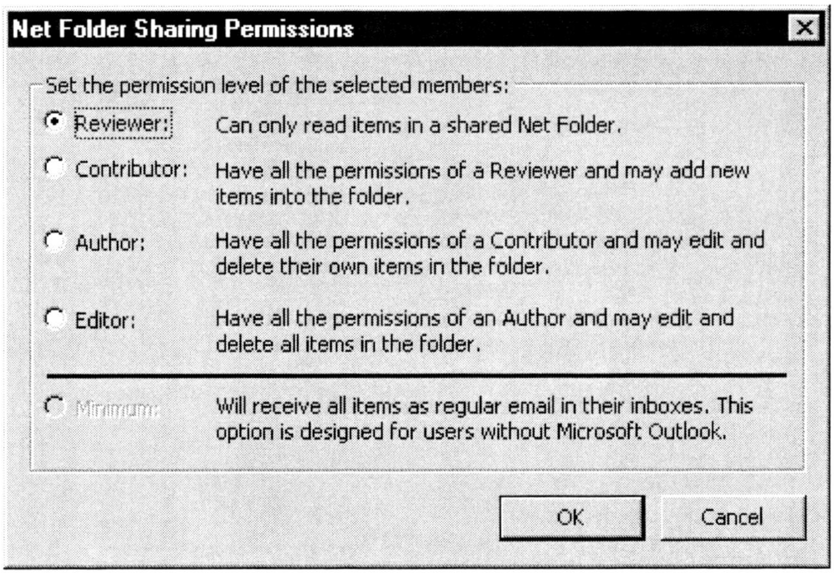

If a potential subscriber does not use Outlook, set his or her permission to Minimum.

16. Click Next.
17. If desired, type a description of the Net Folder.
18. Click Finish.
19. Click OK.

TRY IT 2–4 — PUBLISH A NET FOLDER

In this exercise, you will add your class partner to the Contacts folder, publish the Calendar folder as a Net Folder, and set a permission level for your class partner.

This exercise assumes that you and a class partner have an e-mail address, and you have the Net Folders component installed on your computer. Normally you would create a Net Folder for someone outside your network, but for classroom purposes you will create a Net Folder for your class partner to use.

1. **If necessary, add your class partner to the Contacts folder.**

2. **Copy the Calendar folder to your personal folder.**

RIGHT-CLICK: **Calendar** in the Folder list.

CLICK: **Copy "Calendar"** on the shortcut menu.

The Copy Folder dialog box appears.

CLICK: **Personal Folders**

CLICK: **OK**

3. **Publish the Calendar folder.**

CLICK: **File** on the menu bar.

THEN: Point to **Share** on the File menu.

CLICK: **This Folder**

The Net Folder Wizard appears.

CLICK: **Next**

The next dialog box of the Net Folder Wizard appears.

CLICK: The **Add** button.

CLICK: The Show Names from the drop-down arrow, and click **Contacts**.

Your list of contacts appears.

CLICK: Your class partner's name in the list.

CLICK: The **To** button.

CLICK: **OK**

Your class partner is set up to be a potential subscriber.

4. **Assign a permission level.**

TIP

You can set the same permission to multiple potential subscribers by adding their names to the Member List, selecting their names in the Member List box, and then setting a level of permission.

CLICK: Your class partner's name in the Member List box, if necessary.

CLICK: The **Permissions** button.

THEN: Assign the Contributor permission level to your class partner.

CLICK: **OK**

Your class partner will only be able to read and create items in the Calendar.

CLICK: **Next**

TYPE: [Your name]**'s Calendar**

CLICK: **Next**

CLICK: **Finish**

An alert box appears, telling you that you have sent your invitation successfully.

CLICK: **OK**

5. **Display your Inbox.**

6. **Accept your class partner's invitation.**

CLICK: The **Send/Receive** button on the toolbar, if necessary.

DOUBLE-CLICK: The message that contains the subject *New subscription to [class partner's name]*.

A window appears, describing the subscription.

CLICK: The **Accept** button.

An alert box appears informing you that you have accepted the invitation for the Net Folder for your class partner's calendar.

CLICK: **OK**

Your class partner's calendar is now displayed in your Folder List.

7. **Add an appointment to your class partner's Calendar.**

CLICK: Your class partner's Calendar in the Folder List.

THEN: Display tomorrow's date.

CLICK: The 11:00 A.M. line.

TYPE: [Your name]**'s meeting with the president**.

Outlook will automatically display this addition in your class partner's Personal Folders Calendar in 30 minutes. For classroom purposes, you will send the update now.

8. **Send the update to your class partner's Calendar now.**

RIGHT-CLICK: [Your class partner]'s Calendar in the Folder List.

CLICK: **Properties**

The [your class partner]'s Calendar Properties dialog box appears.

CLICK: The **Sharing** tab.

Notice that Outlook will automatically send updates every 30 minutes.

TIP

You can specify Outlook to send updates at a time interval other than 30 minutes. Click the Updates will be sent out every drop-down arrow, and click a time interval.

CLICK: The **Send Updates Now** button.

An alert box appears, informing you that the updates were sent successfully.

CLICK: **OK** twice.

9. **View the update.**

CLICK: Your Calendar under Personal Folders, and display tomorrow's date.

Your Calendar should look similar to the following:

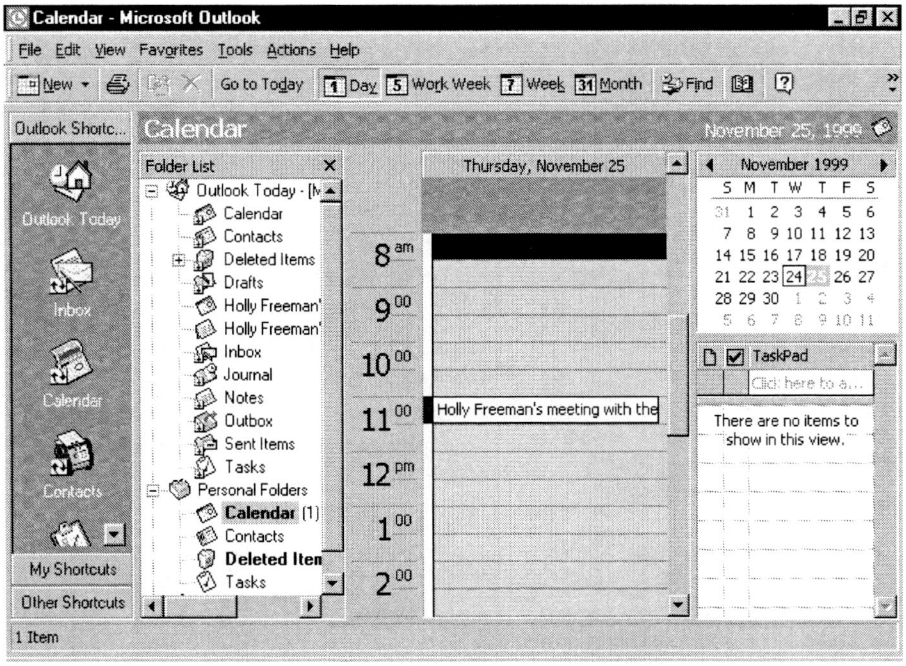

WORKING OFFLINE

For Your Information

If you work chiefly with Exchange Server, you probably know that there are times that you need or want to use Outlook *offline*—that is, when Outlook is not connected to the server. Perhaps the server is down for servicing, or you want to use Outlook when you are traveling. Whatever your reasons are, Outlook lets you work offline.

Creating an Offline File Folder

To work with Outlook both on Exchange Server and offline, you must first create an offline folder file (OST file). An OST file is essentially a copy of all of your Outlook folders. By creating an OST file, you provide a way for Exchange Server to track both your offline and online folders.

To create an offline folder file:

1. Click the Inbox.

2. Click Tools on the menu bar.

3. Click Services on the Tools menu.

4. If necessary, click Microsoft Exchange Server in the The following information services are set up in this profile box.

5. Click the Properties button.

6. Click the Advanced tab to display the Microsoft Exchange Server dialog box.

❼ Click the Offline Folder File Settings button to display the Offline Folder File Settings dialog box.

❽ Click OK three times.

Setting Outlook to Work Offline

To work offline, you must tell Exchange Server that you want to work in Outlook without connecting to the server.

To work offline:

❶ If necessary, set up an OST folder file.

❷ Quit Outlook.

❸ Start Outlook.

❹ In the Microsoft Exchange Server dialog box (as shown below), click the Work Offline button.

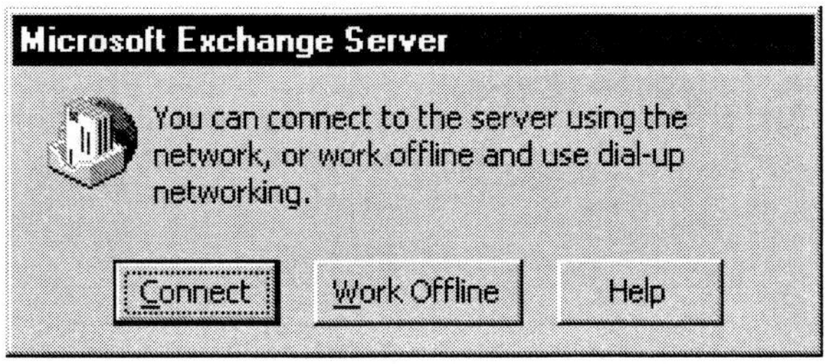

❺ Use Outlook as you would normally.

TRY IT 2–5 — WORK OFFLINE

In this exercise, you will create an offline folder file, set Outlook to work offline, and add a task to the Tasks folder.

---

1. Create an offline file folder.

CLICK: The Inbox.

CLICK: **Tools** on the menu bar.

CLICK: **Services** on the Tools menu.

The Services dialog box appears. Notice that Microsoft Exchange Server is already selected.

CLICK: The **Properties** button.

CLICK: The **Advanced** tab.

The Microsoft Exchange Server dialog box appears.

CLICK: The **Offline Folder File Settings** button.

The Offline Folder File Settings dialog box appears. Notice where the OST file will be stored.

CLICK: **OK** three times.

TIP

You can specify Outlook to ask you to choose a connection type every time you start Outlook. Click **Tools** on the menu bar, click **Services** on the Tools menu, click **Microsoft Exchange Server** in the The following information services are set up in this profile box, click **Properties**, click the **General** tab, and select the **Choose the connection type when starting** check box.

2. **Set Outlook to work offline.**

FIRST: Quit Outlook.

If an alert box appears, telling you that Outlook is going to synchronize your files, click OK.

THEN: Start Outlook.

CLICK: The **Work Offline** button.

Outlook is now offline.

3. **Add a task.**

FIRST: Display the Tasks folder.

TYPE: **Create presentation on mountaineering.** in the Click here to add a new Task text box.

PRESS: **Enter**

The task is created offline.

4. **Quit Outlook.**

Synchronizing Folders

After you make changes to a folder offline, you will then need to update the online folder that's on the server. You can tell Outlook to *synchronize* the offline folder with the online folder so that the folders will contain the same information. Depending on your settings, Outlook will automatically synchronize your offline folders when you set Outlook to work online at start up. Outlook can synchronize one folder at a time, or all of the folders at once.

To manually synchronize a folder:

1. Set Outlook to work online.
2. Display the Folder List.
3. Click the folder that you want to synchronize.
4. Click Tools on the menu bar.
5. Point to Synchronize on the Tools menu.
6. Click This Folder.

To synchronize all folders:

1. Set Outlook to work online.
2. Click Tools on the menu bar.
3. Point to Synchronize on the Tools menu.
4. Click All Folders.

> You can also synchronize all Outlook folders by pressing F9.

Creating a Quick Synchronization Group

If you want to synchronize more than one folder at a time, and you don't want to synchronize every folder in Outlook, you can select certain folders to comprise a group of folders that you can synchronize. When you want to synchronize a group, simply click the group folder.

To create a quick synchronization group:

1. Click Tools on the menu bar.
2. Point to Synchronize.
3. Click Offline Folder Settings.
4. Click the Quick Synchronization tab, and click New to display the Quick Synchronization Group dialog box as shown below:

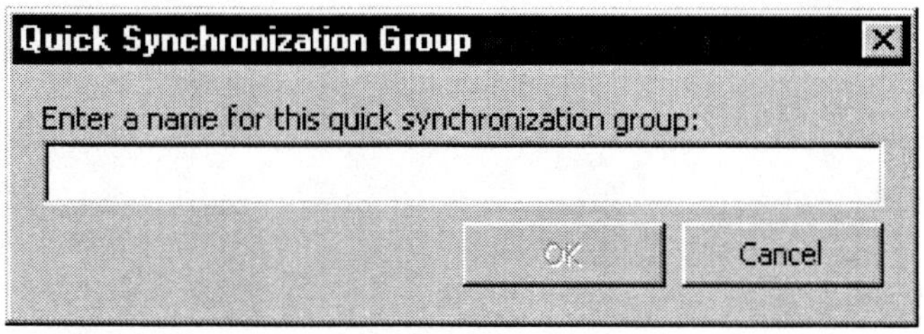

5. Type the name for the group, and click OK.
6. Select the name of the new group, and click Choose Folders.
7. If necessary, click the plus sign to the left of the folder type.
8. Select the check box to the left of each folder you want to include in the group.
9. Click OK twice.

Synchronizing by Message Size

If you don't want to download large messages onto your computer during synchronization, you can specify a maximum amount of kilobytes per message that you will allow Outlook to download. The messages that have more kilobytes than specified will be moved to the Large Messages folder on your server.

To synchronize by message size:

1. Click Tools on the menu bar.
2. Point to Synchronize.
3. Click Offline Folder Settings.
4. Click the Download Options button to display the Download Options dialog box, as shown below:

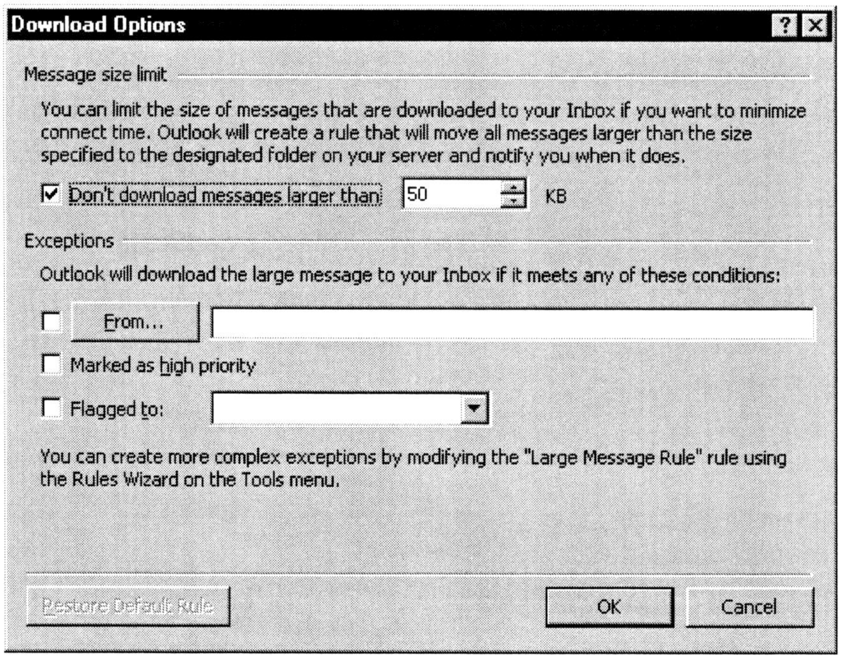

❺ In the Message size limit section, specify the maximum number of kilobytes in a message that you want to download by clicking the up or down arrows, or by selecting the number in the text box and typing a new number.

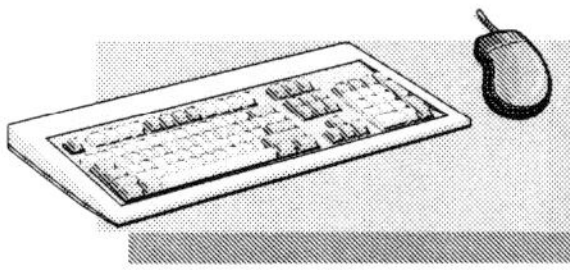

TRY IT 2–6 — SYNCHRONIZE FOLDERS

In this exercise, you will set Outlook to work online and then synchronize the Tasks folder. You will then create a quick synchronization group that includes the Inbox, Calendar folder, and the Contacts folder. Finally, you will specify the maximum amount of kilobytes per message that you will allow Outlook to download.

---

1. **Start Outlook and set it to work online.**

2. **Display the Tasks Folder.**

   Notice that the task you added is not on your task list.

3. **Synchronize your Tasks folder with the online folder.**

   Depending on your connection speed and settings, Outlook might automatically synchronize your Tasks folder.

   CLICK: **Tools** on the menu bar.

   THEN: Point to **Synchronize** on the Tools menu.

   CLICK: **This Folder**

   The Tasks folder is synchronized. The task you created in the previous exercise now appears in the task list.

4. **Create a quick synchronization group.**

   CLICK: **Tools** on the menu bar.

   THEN: Point to **Synchronize**.

   CLICK: **Offline Folder Settings**

   The Offline Folder Settings dialog box appears.

CLICK: The **Quick Synchronization** tab, and click the **New** button.

TYPE: **Inbox/Cal/Contact**

CLICK: **OK**

The new group is already selected.

CLICK: The **Choose Folders** button.

The Choose Folders dialog box appears.

THEN: If necessary, click the plus sign to the left of Mailbox.

NEXT: Select the check boxes to the left of the Calendar Contacts, and Inbox folders.

CLICK: **OK** twice.

The group is created.

5. **Restart Outlook and work offline.**

6. **Create a contact using the following information:**

Full Name:	Hi Knowles
Company:	Rocky Mountain Hikes
E-mail:	hik@rmh.com

7. **Create an appointment using the following information:**

Day:	Next Saturday
Time:	4:00 PM
Subject:	Attend Hi Knowles's Rock Climbing Presentation

8. **Restart Outlook and work online.**

9. **Synchronize the group.**

CLICK: **Tools** on the menu bar.

THEN: Point to **Synchronize** on the Tools menu.

CLICK: **Inbox/Cal/Contact**

The group is synchronized.

10. Synchronize by message size.

CLICK: **Tools** on the menu bar.

THEN: Point to **Synchronize**.

CLICK: **Offline Folder Settings**

The Offline Folder Settings dialog box appears.

CLICK: The **Download Options** button.

The Download Options dialog box appears.

THEN: In the Message size limit section, select the current number.

TYPE: **800**

CLICK: **OK** twice.

Outlook will not download any messages that are more than 800 KB during synchronization.

Importing and Exporting Data

For Your Information

You can import files from other programs into Outlook, and conversely, you can export files from Outlook into other programs. This is especially useful if you used to use a different mail program, then switched to Outlook. You can easily import contacts from the other mail program into the Contacts folder.

Importing and Exporting Files

The steps to import vs. the steps to export files are similar. You use the Import and Export Wizard to import and export files.

To import a file from another mail program:

❶ Click File on the menu bar.

❷ Click Import and Export on the File menu to display the Import and Export Wizard, as shown in the figure below:

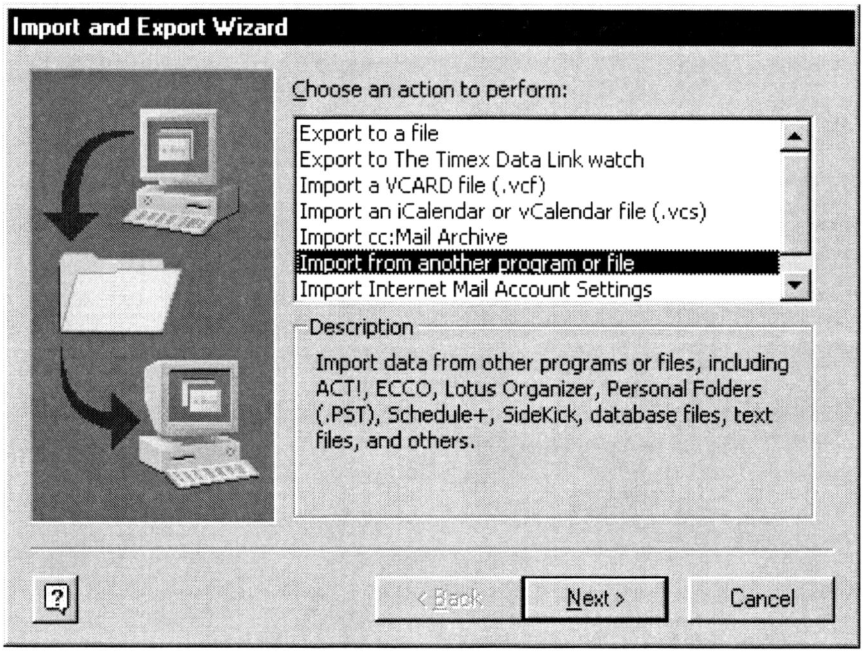

❸ Click Import Internet Mail and Addresses.

❹ Click Next to display the next wizard dialog box, as shown below:

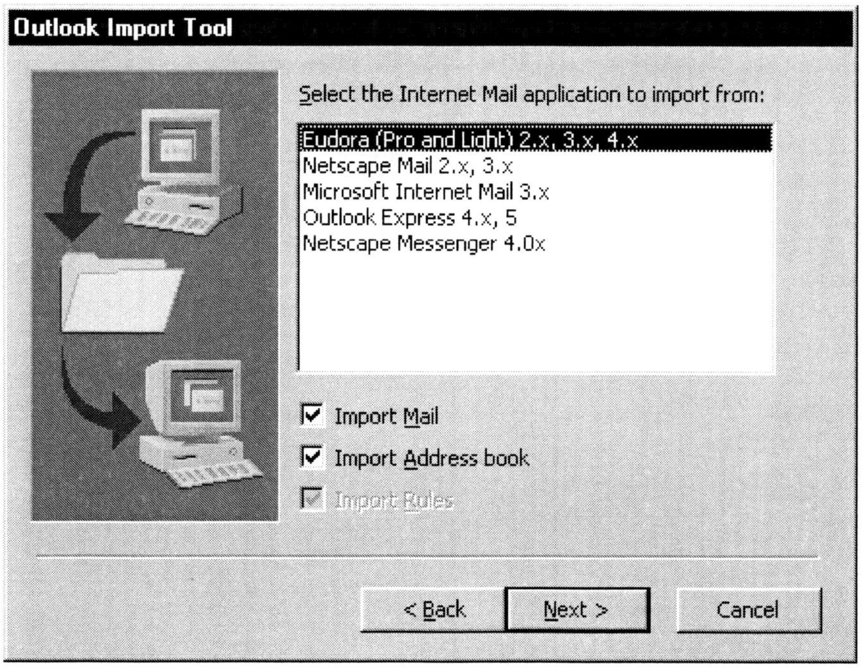

❺ Click the name of the mail program files you want to import.

❻ Click Next to display the final wizard dialog box, as shown on the next page.

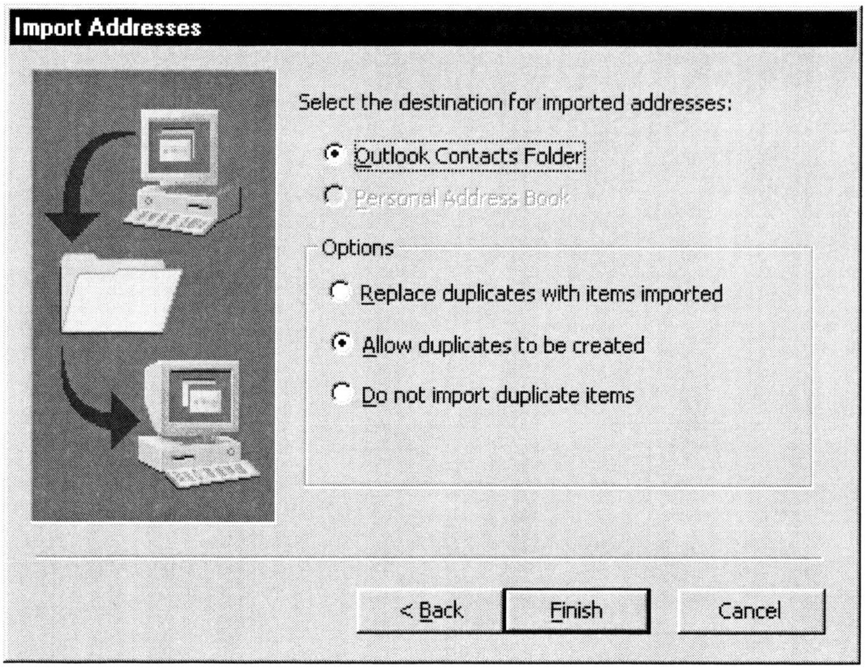

❼ Click Finish.

❽ Click OK.

To export a file to another file:

❶ Click File on the menu bar.

❷ Click Import and Export on the File menu.

❸ Click Export to a file.

❹ Click Next.

❺ Click Personal Folder File (.pst).

❻ Click Next.

❼ Click a folder that you want to export.

❽ Click Next.

❾ If desired, type a file name in the Save exported file as text box.

❿ If desired, click the Browse button to navigate to a folder to put the file in.

⓫ Click Finish.

⓬ Click OK.

TRY IT 2–7 — IMPORT A FILE FROM OUTLOOK EXPRESS

In this exercise, you will create a contact in Outlook Express, then import the file into Outlook.

---

1. **Create a contact in Outlook Express.**

FIRST: Open Outlook Express.

CLICK: The **Addresses** 

button on the toolbar.

The Address Book appears.

CLICK: The **New** 

button on the Address Book toolbar.

CLICK: **New Contact**

TYPE: **Ben Lynn**

THEN: In the E-mail Address text box, type **Benl@company.com**.

CLICK: The **Add** button.

The contact is created.

CLICK: The **Close**  button on the top-right corner of the Address Book.

THEN: Close Outlook Express.

2. **Import the contact into Outlook.**

CLICK: **File** on the menu bar.

CLICK: **Import and Export** on the File menu.

The Import and Export Wizard is displayed.

CLICK: **Import Internet Mail and Addresses**

CLICK: **Next**

The next wizard dialog box is displayed.

CLICK: **Outlook Express 4.x, 5**

THEN: Clear the **Import Mail** and **Import Rules** check boxes.

CLICK: **Next**

The final wizard dialog box is displayed. Notice that the Outlook Contacts folder is already selected to be the place where the imported files will be stored.

CLICK: The Replace duplicates with items imported option.

CLICK: **Finish**

The Import progress dialog box appears, showing a progress bar as the file is imported. Then the Import Summary dialog box appears, displaying the results of the import.

CLICK: **OK**

THEN: Display the Contacts Folder.

Ben Lynn now appears in your Contacts folder.

Another use for Outlook Express is sending e-mail messages to a *newsgroup*. A newsgroup is a collection of messages that are constantly being sent and responded to by people within the group. Each newsgroup discusses a specific topic, such as gardening, rock bands, or television programs. These messages are posted on a *news server*. A news server is a computer that is maintained by a company, group, or individual, and is configured to accept messages from newsgroups. (Your Internet Service provider most likely has a news server you can connect to.) In order to read these posted messages, you must use a *newsreader*. A newsreader is an application that enables you to send and receive newsgroup messages. You access a newsreader using Outlook Express.

To access the newsreader from Outlook, click View on the menu bar, point to Go To, and click News. Outlook Express will open. Under the Newsgroups section, click the Setup a Newsgroup account link. (You will only have to do this once.) Follow the steps in the Internet Connection Wizard. (You will need to know your ISP's NNTP server name to successfully set up the account.)

After you set up the account, an alert box will appear, asking you to download the newsgroups from the news account you just added. Click Yes. (This will take a few minutes; however, you will only have to do this once.) After the newsgroups are downloaded, the Newsgroups Subscriptions dialog box will appear. This is where you choose or *subscribe* to a newsgroup. Simply type a topic in the Display newsgroups which contain text box to view a list of newsgroups that concern the specified topic, and click a newsgroup in the list. If you want to join the group, click the Subscribe button. If you want to just view the group, click the Go to button. In either case, the newsreader will appear, and the messages from the newsgroup will download onto your computer.

To send a message to the newsgroup, click the New Post button on the toolbar, type a subject and a message, and click the Send button.

To reply to a message, click the message that you want to reply to, and click the Reply Group button (so that the message can be seen by the newsgroup), or click the Reply button (to only send the message to the person who posted it).

QuickLook at Lesson 2

To	Do This
Create a shared folder	**1.** From any private folder, click **File** on the menu bar. **2.** Point to **New** on the File menu, then click Folder. **3.** In the Name box, type a name. **4.** Click the Folder Contains drop-down arrow, and then click the type of item the folder will contain. **5.** In the Select where to place the folder box, click the plus sign to the left of Public Folders, then click All Public Folders. **6.** Click **OK**. **7.** Click **Yes** or **No** in the alert box that appears.
Grant permissions to folders	**1.** Display the Folder List. **2.** Right-click the folder. **3.** Click **Properties** on the shortcut menu. **4.** Click the **Permissions** tab on the Properties dialog box. **5.** Click the **Add** button. **6.** Type or click the name of the person to be added to the permissions list. **7.** Click the **Add** button. **8.** Click **OK**. **9.** Select the name in the Name list. **10.** Click the Roles drop-down arrow and click a role to determine the level of permission assigned to each user. **11.** Click **OK**.
Grant delegate access	**1.** Click **Tools** on the menu bar. **2.** Click **Options** on the Tools menu. **3.** Click the **Delegates** tab. **4.** Click the **Add** button. **5.** Type or click the name of the delegate. **6.** Click the **Add** button. **7.** Click **OK**. **8.** Select the appropriate permissions for the desired folders. **9.** Click **OK** twice.

To	Do This
Publish a Net Folder and set permissions	**1.** Display the Folder List. **2.** If desired, create a folder that you want to share in the Personal Folders file. *Or* Copy an existing folder to your Personal Folders File. **3.** Click the folder that you want to share. **4.** Click **File** on the menu bar. **5.** Point to **Share** on the File menu. **6.** Click **This Folder**. **7.** If desired, close the Office Assistant. **8.** Click **Next**. **9.** Click the **Add** button. **10.** Click the Show Names from the drop-down arrow and click **Contacts**. **11.** Type the name of the potential subscriber in the Type Name or Select from List box. *Or* Select the name from the list. **12.** Click the **To** button. **13.** Click **OK**. **14.** Click a name in the Member List box, if necessary. **15.** Click the Permissions button and assign a level of permission to the potential subscriber in the Net Folder Sharing Permissions dialog box. **16.** Click **Next**. **17.** If desired, type a description of the Net Folder. **18.** Click **Finish**. **19.** Click **OK**.
Create an offline folder file	**1.** Click the Inbox. **2.** Click **Tools** on the menu bar. **3.** Click **Services** on the Tools menu. **4.** Click **Microsoft Exchange Server** in the The following information services are set up in this profile box, if necessary. **5.** Click the **Properties** button. **6.** Click the **Advanced** tab to display the Microsoft Exchange Server dialog box. **7.** Click the **Offline Folder File Settings** button to display the Offline Folder File Settings dialog box. **8.** Click OK three times.

To	Do This
Work offline	**1.** If necessary, set up an OST folder file. **2.** Quit Outlook. **3.** Start Outlook. **4.** In the Microsoft Exchange Server dialog box, click the **Work Offline** button.
Manually synchronize a folder	**1.** Set Outlook to work online. **2.** Display the Folder List. **3.** Click the folder that you want to synchronize. **4.** Click **Tools** on the menu bar. **5.** Point to **Synchronize** on the Tools menu. **6.** Click **This Folder**.
Synchronize all folders	**1.** Set Outlook to work online. **2.** Click **Tools** on the menu bar. **3.** Point to **Synchronize** on the Tools menu. **4.** Click **All Folders**.
Create a quick synchronization group	**1.** Click **Tools** on the menu bar. **2.** Point to **Synchronize**. **3.** Click **Offline Folder Settings**. **4.** Click the **Quick Synchronization** tab, and click **New**. **5.** Type the name for the group, and click **OK**. **6.** Select the name of the new group, and click **Choose Folders**. **7.** If necessary, click the plus sign to the left of the folder type. **8.** Select the check box to the left of each folder you want to include in the group. **9.** Click **OK** twice.
Synchronize by message size	**1.** Click **Tools** on the menu bar. **2.** Point to **Synchronize**. **3.** Click **Offline Folder Settings**. **4.** Click **Download Options**. **5.** In the Message size limit section, specify the maximum number of kilobytes in a message that you want to download by clicking the up or down arrows, or by selecting the number in the text box, and typing a new number.

To	Do This
Import a file from another mail program	**1.** Click **File** on the menu bar. **2.** Click **Import and Export** on the File menu. **3.** Click **Import Internet Mail and Addresses**. **4.** Click **Next**. **5.** Click the name of the mail program files you want to import. **6.** Click **Next**. **7.** Click **Finish**. **8.** Click **OK**.
Export a file to another file	**1.** Click **File** on the menu bar. **2.** Click **Import and Export** on the File menu. **3.** Click **Export to a file**. **4.** Click **Next**. **5.** Click **Personal Folder File (.pst)**. **6.** Click **Next**. **7.** Click a folder that you want to export. **8.** Click **Next**. **9.** If desired, type a file name in the Save exported file as text box. **10.** If desired, click the **Browse** button to navigate to a folder to put the file in. **11.** Click **Finish**. **12.** Click **OK**.

SkillCheck – Lesson 2

1. Make the Contacts folder a public folder.
2. Grant delegate access to the Contacts folder to your class partner, and set the permission level to Editor.
3. Create a folder called LMR Tasks, and put the task "Create presentation on mountaineering" in it.
4. Publish the LMR Tasks folder as a Net Folder, and give your class partner the Contributor permission level.
5. While working offline, create a note about going to the dentist.
6. Connect to the server, and then synchronize the Notes folder.
7. Create a quick synchronization group called Task/Journ, and add the Tasks and Journal folder to the group.
8. Export the Tasks folder to the Outlook Intermediate folder.

Answers to the SkillChecks can be found here: **http://www.activeed.com/skanswers/outlook2.htm**

Performance Objectives

You will learn how to:

- Manage mail messages
- Archive mail messages
- Create a signature and a vCard
- Use the Address Book
- Use mail templates

For Your Information

Outlook lets you manage your e-mail messages in many ways. You can organize messages by using the *Rules Wizard.* The Rules Wizard lets you set conditions that will automatically perform actions on messages (such as automatically forwarding specified messages to someone). You can also organize messages by sorting and tracking them.

Using the Rules Wizard to Organize Mail

When you use the Rules Wizard, you create *rules* for messages. Rules consist of three elements—conditions, actions, and exceptions—that when combined, process and organize messages in a certain way. When you create a rule you must describe a condition and an action; however, describing an exception is not required.

The human resources manager at Lakewood Mountain Resort placed an ad in the newspaper for a cook. The ad instructed applicants to e-mail their resumes to her. To quickly separate her general e-mail from the many applicants' e-mails, the human resource manager created a rule that stated that any messages that she receives that contain the word "cook" in the message body (condition), will be automatically sent to a folder called Cook Position (action), except if the message is marked with high importance (exception).

To use the Rules Wizard:

❶ Display the Inbox.

❷ Click Tools on the menu bar.

❸ Click Rules Wizard on the Tools menu.

❹ Click the New button to display the Rules Wizard dialog box, shown on the following page.

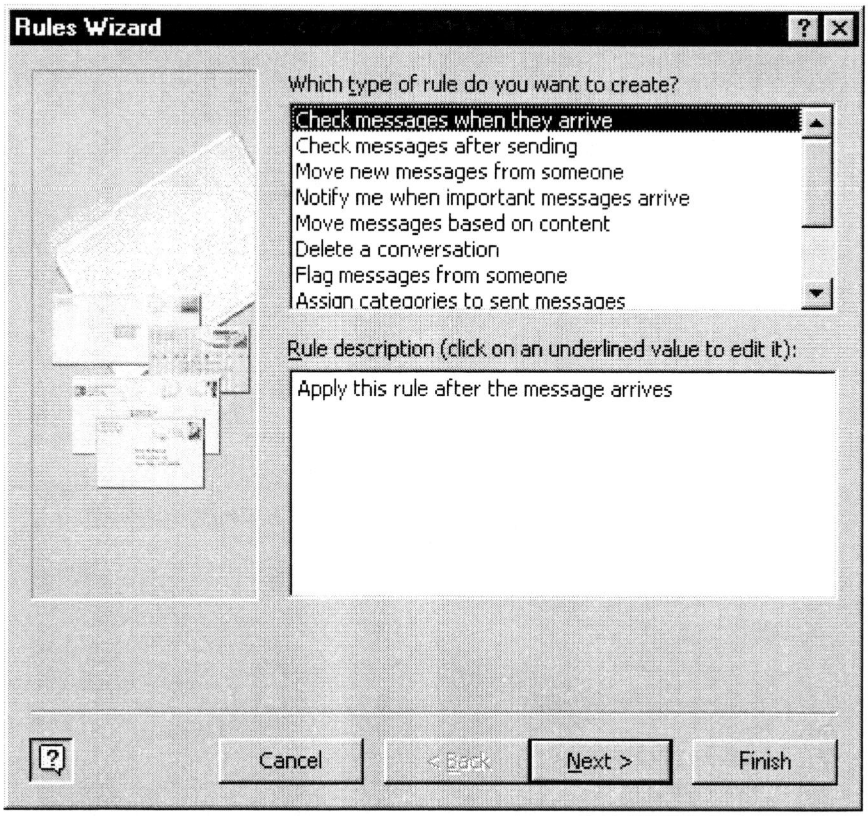

❺ Follow the Rules Wizard instructions, clicking Next after completing each dialog box.

❻ When you are finished specifying options, click Finish.

TRY IT 3–1 — USE THE RULES WIZARD

In this exercise, you will create a rule that puts messages that have the word "cook" in the message body into a folder called "Cook Position," except if the messages are marked with high importance.

---

1. **If necessary, display the Inbox.**
2. **Set the condition of the rule.**

   CLICK: **Tools** on the menu bar.

   CLICK: **Rules Wizard** on the Tools menu.

   The Rules Wizard dialog box appears.

CLICK: The **New** button.

The option Check messages when they arrive is already selected.

If the Office Assistant appears, asking if you want help, click No, don't provide help now.

CLICK: The **Next** button.

The next wizard dialog box appears, asking what condition(s) you want to set.

THEN: Scroll down and select the with specific words in the subject check box.

NEXT: In the Rule description list, click the **specific words** link.

The Search Text dialog box appears, as shown below:

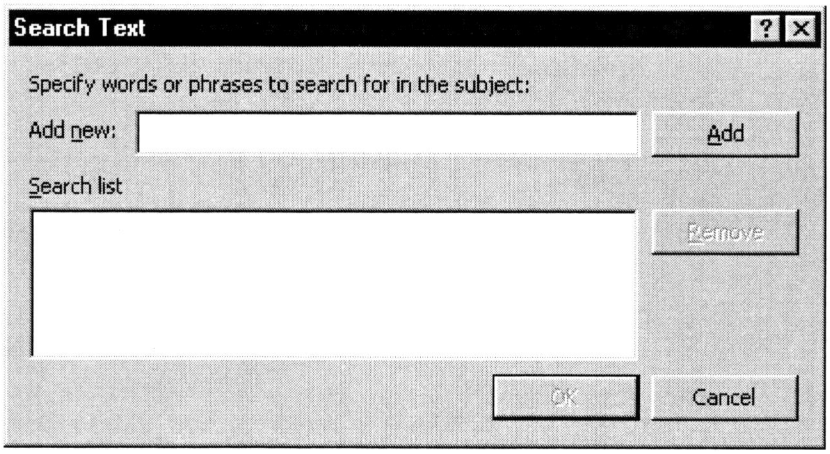

TYPE: **cook**

CLICK: The **Add** button.

CLICK: **OK**

CLICK: **Next**

The next wizard dialog box appears asking what you want to do with the messages.

3. Set the action of the rule.

FIRST: Select the move it to the specified folder check box.

NEXT: In the Rule description list, click the **specified** link.

The Rules Wizard dialog box appears, displaying Outlook folders.

CLICK: The **New** button.

The Create New Folder dialog box appears, as shown in the figure below:

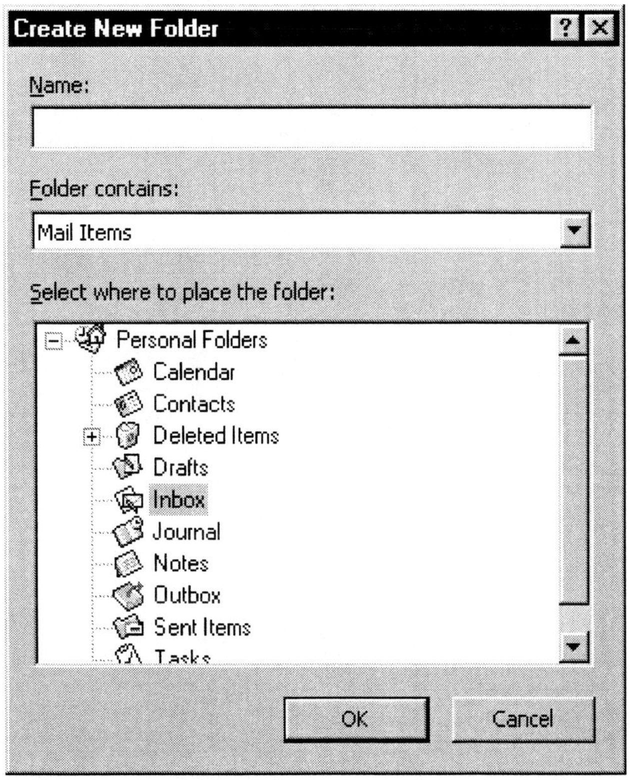

TYPE: **Cook Position**

CLICK: **OK**

An alert box appears, asking if you want to create a shortcut to the folder on the Outlook bar.

CLICK: **Yes**

The folder Cook Position is added to the Outlook bar, and is now selected in the Rules Wizard dialog box.

CLICK: **OK**

CLICK: **Next**

The next wizard dialog box appears, asking you to add an exception (if desired).

4. Set the exception to the rule.

FIRST: Scroll down and select the except if it is marked as importance check box.

NEXT: In the Rules description list, click the importance link.

The Importance dialog box appears, as shown in the figure below:

CLICK: The drop-down arrow, and click **High**.

CLICK: **OK**

CLICK: **Next**

The final wizard dialog box appears asking you to name the Rule. The word "cook" is already displayed.

CLICK: **Finish**

CLICK: **OK**

The rule is created.

TIP

You can run a newly created rule on messages already in the Inbox. Simply select the Run this rule now on messages already in Inbox check box in the last Rule Wizard dialog box.

5. **Test the rule.**

CLICK: The **New Mail Message** button.

A message window appears.

TYPE: Your e-mail address in the To text box.

CLICK: The Subject text box, and type **Cook**.

CLICK: The **Send** button.

The message is sent to you.

CLICK: The **Send/Receive** button.

The message is received. Notice that it appears in the Inbox for only a moment, then it is moved to the Cook Position folder.

You might have to wait a few seconds and click the Send/Receive button again if the message does not appear after the first time you click it.

CLICK: The **My shortcuts** button on the Outlook bar.

CLICK: The **Cook Position** folder.

The cook e-mail appears in the Cook Position folder.

6. **Test the rule again, by creating an e-mail with high importance.**

CLICK: The **New Mail Message** button.

A message window appears.

TYPE: Your e-mail address in the To text box.

CLICK: The Subject text box, and type **Cook**.

THEN: If necessary, click the **More Buttons** button on the toolbar.

CLICK: The **Importance: High** button.

The message is now of high importance.

CLICK: The **Send** button.

The message is sent to you.

CLICK: The **Send/Receive** 

button.

The message is received. Notice that it is not displayed in the Cook Position folder.

THEN: Display the Inbox.

The cook e-mail appears in the Inbox.

Sorting Mail Messages

In Lesson 1, you sorted items within categories. You clicked a column heading such as Full Name or Company to display the items related to that heading in ascending or descending order. You can use the same method for sorting e-mail messages.

You can sort messages in many ways, such as by attachment, by importance, by subject, by when it was received, and so on. Suppose you wanted to quickly find a message that all you really knew about it was that it was sent late yesterday. You could sort the messages by the date and time it was received in descending order so that all the most recently sent items would appear at the top of the list; thus narrowing your search.

To sort mail messages:

- Click the column heading that you want to sort by to toggle between ascending and descending order.

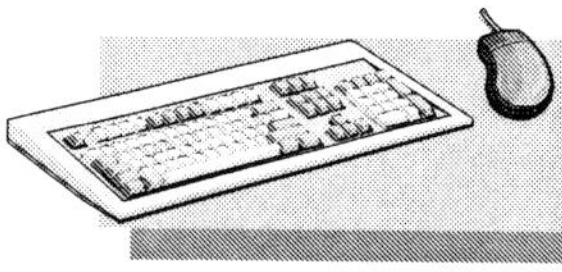

TRY IT 3–2 — SORT MESSAGES

In this exercise, you will sort messages by attachment, sender, subject, and the day and time it was received.

1. **Sort by Attachment.**

   CLICK: The Attachment column heading. (It looks like a paper clip.)

   The message that has an attachment is displayed at the top of the list.

CLICK: The Attachment column heading again.

The messages that have attachments are displayed at the bottom of the list and are sorted in descending order.

2. **Sort by who the message is from.**

CLICK: The From column heading.

The messages are sorted by who sent the message in ascending order. An up arrow appears on the From column heading.

CLICK: The From column heading again.

The messages are sorted by who sent the message in decending order. A down arrow appears on the From column heading.

3. **Sort by Subject.**

CLICK: The Subject column heading.

The messages are sorted by subject in ascending order. An up arrow appears on the Subject column heading.

4. **Sort by when the message was received.**

CLICK: The Received column heading.

The messages are sorted by the date and time the messages were received in descending order. A down arrow appears on the Received column heading.

Tracking when Mail Messages Are Delivered or Read

Outlook has a way for you to track what day and time a message was received and read by a recipient. Before you send a message, you can specify to have Outlook display an alert box (shown in the following figure) requesting that the recipient send a *read receipt* (a notice in the form of an e-mail message) verifying the date and time when he or she received and read the message:

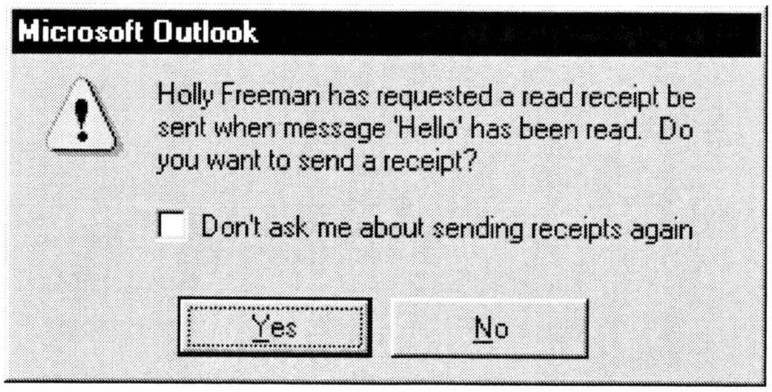

As you can see, the recipient has the choice to accept or decline the request. If the recipient accepts, the following e-mail message will automatically be sent to you after the recipient closes or deletes the message:

```
Your message

    To:   Holly Freeman
    Subject:  Hello
    Sent:   11/2/99 5:32 PM

was read on 11/2/99 5:33 PM.
```

Read receipts verify that the message was received; however, they do not necessarily verify that the messages was read. A recipient could conceivably delete your message without ever reading it—even though the read receipt displays a date and time the message was read.

It's a good idea to read messages that request read receipts because the information in the message is probably important—so important that the sender needs to make sure that you read it and possibly acted upon it as a result of reading it. If you accept to send a read receipt, but you don't really read the message, and as a result a dispute arises, the sender will have proof that he/she sent the message; therefore placing the responsibility solely on you. So if the message said that you were supposed to pick up the boss's mother from the airport and you didn't because you really didn't read the message, then you have only yourself to blame.

To track mail messages:

❶ Create a message, then click the Options button in the message window to display the Message Options dialog box:

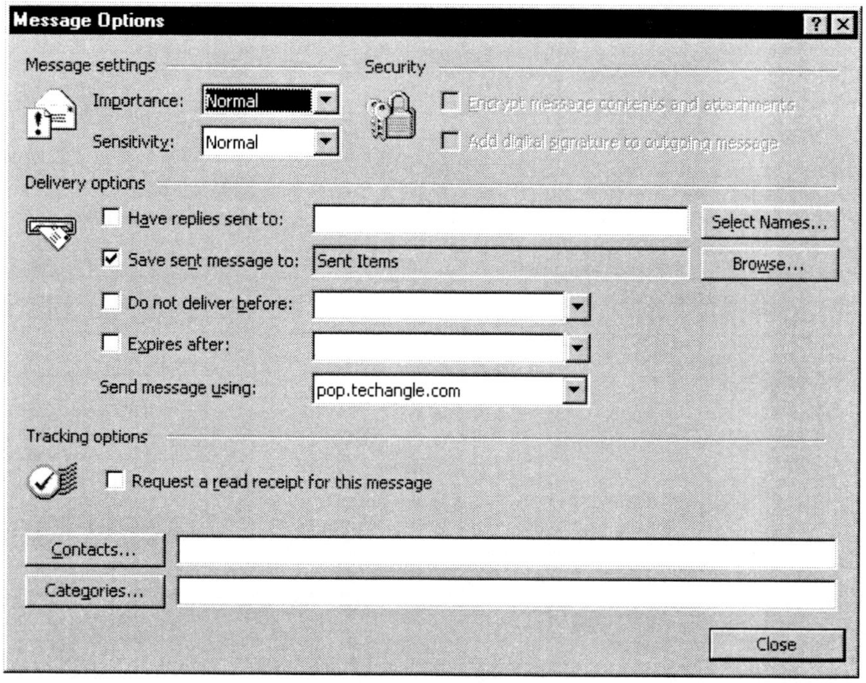

❷ In the Tracking options section, select the Request a read receipt for this message check box.

❸ Click the Close button.

❹ Send the message.

TRY IT 3–3 — TRACK MESSAGES

In this exercise, you will create a message that will request the recipient to send a read receipt after the recipient reads the message.

---

1. Create a message.

CLICK: The **New Mail Message** button on the toolbar.

A message window appears.

TYPE: Your e-mail address.

CLICK: In the Subject text box and type **Urgent!**

CLICK: In the message area and type **Please pick up the boss's mother at the airport at 12:04, Airways, gate 24.**

2. Track the message.

CLICK: The **Options** button.

The Message Options dialog box appears.

THEN: In the Tracking options section, select the Request a read receipt for this message check box.

CLICK: **Close**

CLICK: The **Send** button.

The message is sent to you.

3. Manually send and receive the message you just sent.

The Urgent message appears in your Inbox.

4. Read the message.

DOUBLE-CLICK: The message.

An alert box appears, requesting that you send a read receipt after you read the message.

TIP

You can flag a message so that the recipient will perform a particular action, such as call you or reply to you. Create a message, click the **Flag for Follow Up** button on the toolbar, click the Flag to drop-down arrow, and click a desired flag. If desired, click the Due by drop-down arrow, and click a date. Click **OK**.

CLICK: **Yes**

THEN: Close the message.

5. **Manually send and receive messages.**

The read receipt message appears in your Inbox. Notice that a read receipt icon appears in the Icon column and the word *Read* now appears in front of the subject, Urgent! as shown below:

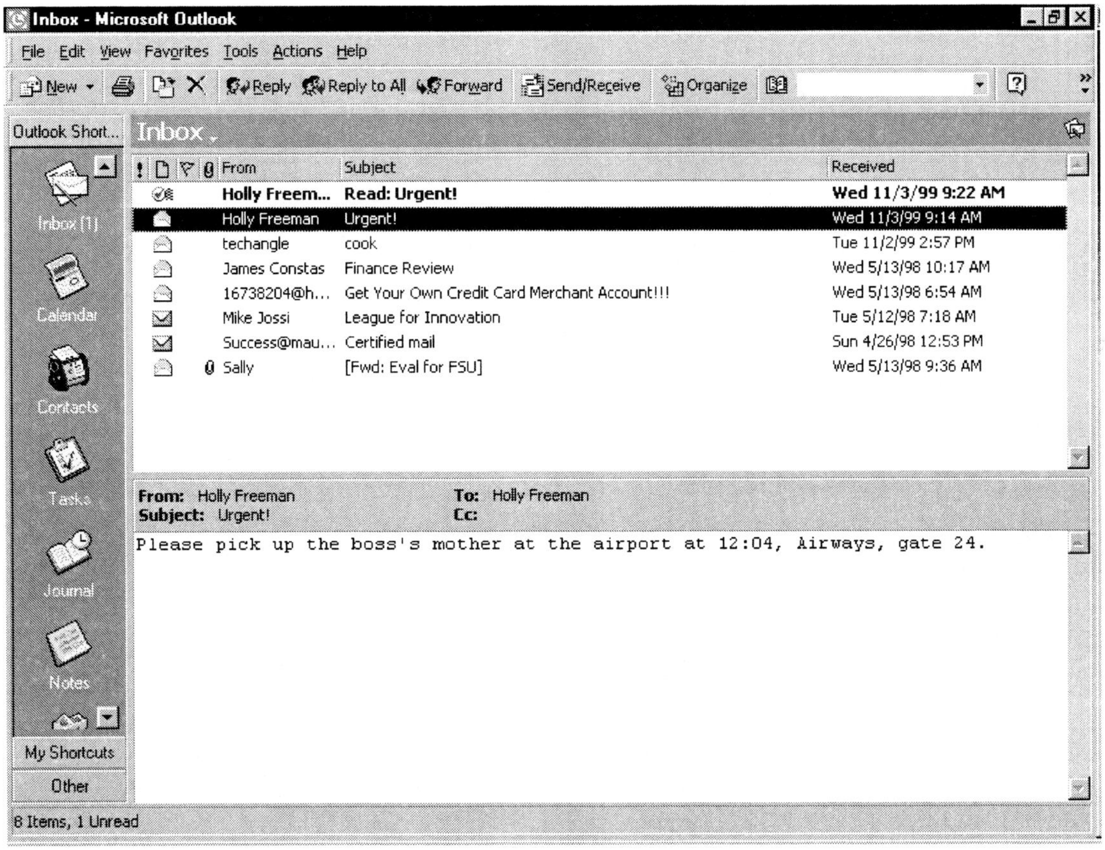

6. Read the read receipt.

DOUBLE-
CLICK: The Read: Urgent! message.

The receipt appears similar to the figure shown below:

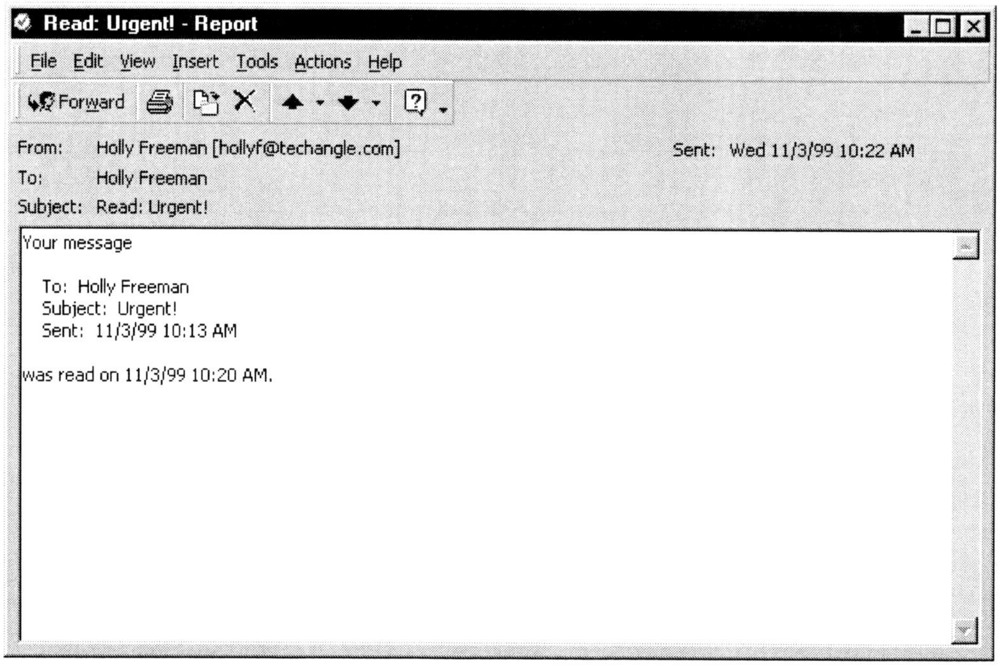

ARCHIVING MAIL MESSAGES

For Your Information

Another way you can manage messages is by *archiving* old messages. Archiving simply means to move old messages into a folder on your hard disk. When you archive outdated messages in a folder, they are removed from your Outlook folder and are copied to a .pst file on your hard drive. Archiving merely helps to remove the clutter from your Outlook folders.

If you send and receive messages frequently, both your Inbox and Sent items folders might contain hundreds of messages over the course of a few months. Although you can delete these messages permanently, it is a good idea to archive the messages, in the event that you should need to access them later.

AutoArchiving Folders

Outlook automatically uses its AutoArchive feature to remove old items to an archive file periodically. Even though Outlook does this automatically, it is helpful to understand the AutoArchive settings and to know where the archived file is stored, in case you need to retrieve it. You can view the default settings for AutoArchiving messages in three locations: the AutoArchive dialog box, the Inbox Properties dialog box, and the Archive dialog box.

To view information about AutoArchive:

❶ Click Tools on the menu bar.

❷ Click Options on the Tools menu.

❸ Click the Other tab.

❹ Click the AutoArchive button to display the AutoArchive dialog box:

Or

❶ Display the Folder List.

❷ Right-click the Inbox folder.

❸ Click Properties.

❹ Click the AutoArchive tab to display the following:

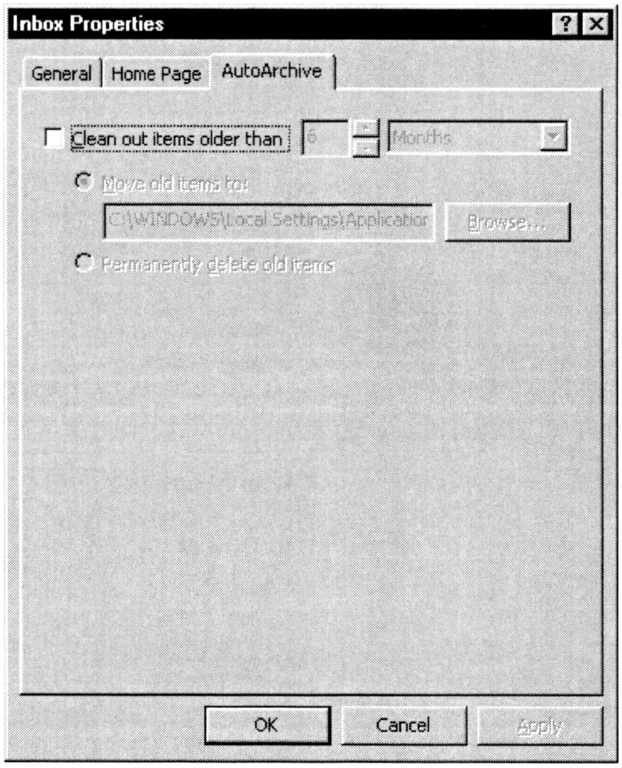

Or

❶ Click File on the menu bar.

❷ Click Archive on the File menu to display the Archive dialog box, as shown in the figure below:

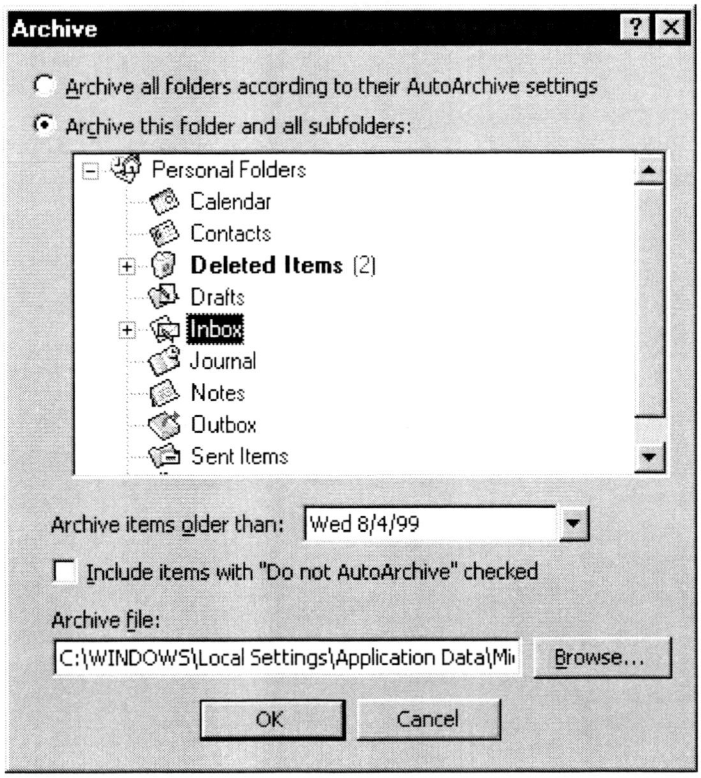

The AutoArchive dialog box includes four settings as shown in the table below:

Setting	What It Does
AutoArchive every [number] days	Each time you start Outlook, it checks to determine when your folders were last archived. The number of days in the setting determines when AutoArchive will next archive your folders. The default is 14 days.
Prompt before AutoArchive	Outlook will notify you before it AutoArchives your folders. You have the option to override the AutoArchive feature if you know that there are still items that you want to keep in your folder.
Delete expired Items when AutoArchiving (e-mail folders only)	Outlook will move outdated e-mail messages to the Deleted Items folder, rather than Archiving them. This option can help prevent filling up your archive file with hundreds of old messages that you would really rather delete and not keep. This option also makes it unnecessary to mark old e-mail for deletion periodically.
Default archive file	Displays the current location of where your archive files are stored. You can change this location if you desire.

The AutoArchive tab in the Inbox Properties dialog box includes the following settings:

Setting	What It Does
Clean out items older than [number] [Months/Weeks/Days]	Specifies the amount of time you want items to remain in a folder before they are archived or deleted.
Move old items to	Displays the current location of where your archive files are stored. You can change this location if you desire.
Permanently delete old items	Permanently removes outdated items.

The Archive dialog box includes the following settings:

Setting	What It Does
Archive all folders according to their AutoArchive settings	All folders are archived using the default AutoArchive settings, or any AutoArchive settings that you have changed.
Archive this folder and all subfolders	Lets you select one Outlook folder to be archived, and any subfolders within this folder.
Archive items older than [date]	Sets the date when items are considered to be outdated in the current folder. This option overrides the AutoArchive settings.
Include items with "Do not AutoArchive" checked	Overrides the "Do not AutoArchive" option.
Archive file	Displays the current location of where your archive files are stored. You can change this location if you desire.

Controlling Archive Settings

You can leave the settings as is or you can change the settings using the three dialog boxes just mentioned. When Outlook automatically archives folders, it uses the default archive settings for each Outlook folder. However, you do not need to rely on AutoArchive when you want to archive folders. You can manually archive folders at any time. If you decide to archive a folder, Outlook will still use the default archive settings, unless you change them.

The table below details the default settings for mail folders:

Folder	Default Archive Setting
Inbox	Items that have been in this folder for more than six months are moved to the archive file.
Outbox	Items that have been in this folder for more than three months are moved to the archive file.
Sent Items	Items that have been in this folder for more than two months are moved to the archive file.

You use the Archive dialog box to manually archive a folder.

To manually archive mail messages:

1. Click File on the menu bar.
2. Click Archive on the File menu.
3. If necessary, click the Archive this folder and all subfolders option.
4. Click a folder.
5. Click the Archive items older than drop-down arrow and select a date.
6. Click OK.

Restoring an Archive File

You don't actually need to restore an archive file; you simply import it.

To restore an archive file:

1. Click File on the menu bar.
2. Click Import and Export on the File menu.
3. Click Next.
4. Scroll down and click Personal Folder File (pst.).
5. Click Next.
6. If necessary, navigate to where your archive file is stored.
7. Click Next.
8. Click the appropriate import options.
9. Click Finish.

TRY IT 3–4 — ARCHIVE MAIL MESSAGES

In this exercise, you will change archive settings for your Inbox, then manually archive the folder using the new settings. Finally, you will import the archived files.

---

1. **Manually archive your Inbox.**

   CLICK: **File** on the menu bar.

   CLICK: **Archive** on the File menu.

   > The Archive dialog box appears. Notice that the Archive this folder and all subfolders option is selected, and the Inbox is selected.

   CLICK: The Archive items older than drop-down arrow, and click tomorrow's date.

   CLICK: The **Browse** button, and navigate to the Outlook Intermediate folder on your hard disk.

   CLICK: **OK** twice.

   > An alert box appears.

   CLICK: **Yes**

   > The Inbox is archived. All messages older than tomorrow's date are archived.

2. **Restore the archive file.**

   CLICK: **File** on the menu bar.

   CLICK: **Import and Export** on the File menu.

   > The Import and Export Wizard appears. Import from another program or file is already selected.

   CLICK: **Next**

   > The next wizard dialog box appears.

THEN: Scroll down, and click **Personal Folder File (.pst)**.

CLICK: **Next**

The next wizard dialog box appears.

CLICK: The **Browse** button.

The Open Personal Folders dialog box appears.

THEN: Navigate to the Outlook Intermediate folder.

DOUBLE-CLICK: **archive**

CLICK: **Next**

The final wizard dialog box appears.

CLICK: **Finish**

The files are restored to your Inbox.

CREATING A SIGNATURE AND A VCARD

For Your Information

You can set up Outlook to automatically insert information such as a *signature* or a *vCard* at the end of your e-mail messages. A signature can be a few lines of information about yourself, such as your job title, your work phone, or a perhaps a nickname. You could also insert a favorite quote as a signature. You can think of a vCard as an electronic business card that has all of your contact information on it. The vCard is inserted as an attachment to your messages.

Adding a Signature to a Message

You can create several different signatures. You could create one for work called "work" that includes your job title, work phone, company name and mission statement. You could create a social signature called "fun" that has your nickname and a favorite quote. Before you send a message, simply click the name you assigned for a particular signature, and send it.

To create a signature:

1. Click Tools on the menu bar.
2. Click Options on the Tools menu.
3. Click the Mail Format tab.
4. In the Signature section, click the Signature Picker button to display the Signature Picker dialog box, shown on the following page.

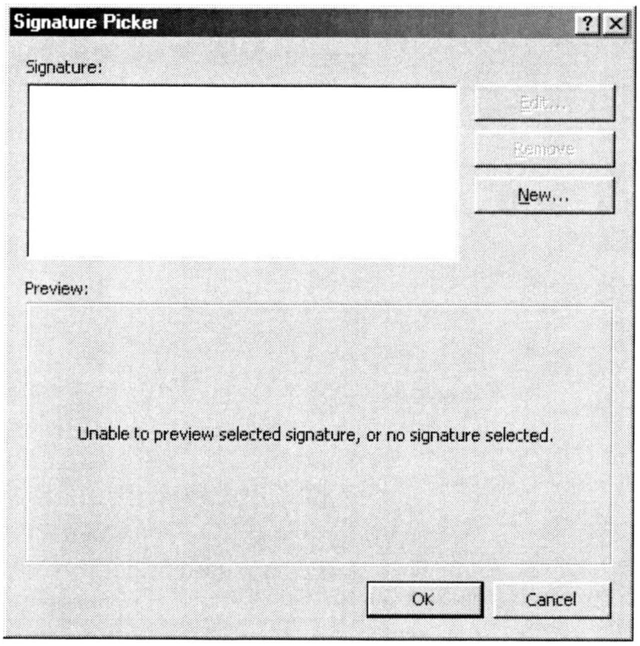

❺ Click the New button to display the Create New Signature dialog box:

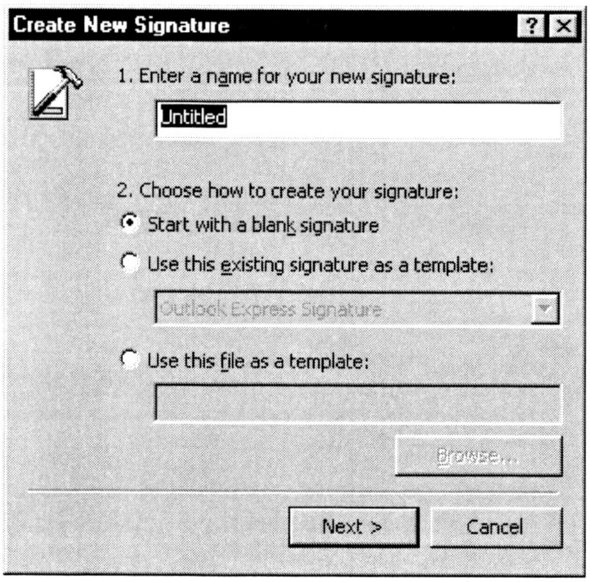

❻ Type a name for the signature.

7. Click Next to display the Edit Signature dialog box:

8. Type the text of the signature.

9. Click Finish.

10. Click OK.

> Notice that the signature that you just created will be the default signature every time you send a message. If you don't want this to be the default, click the drop-down arrow, and click None.

11. Click OK.

To add a signature to a message that doesn't already have one:

1. Create a message.

2. In the message window, click Insert on the menu bar.

3. Point to Signature.

4. Click the signature that you want to use.

TRY IT 3–5 — CREATE A SIGNATURE

In this exercise, you will create a signature, create a message, and send the message with the signature.

---

1. **Create a signature.**

CLICK: **Tools** on the menu bar.

CLICK: **Options** on the Tools menu.

CLICK: The **Mail Format** tab.

THEN: In the Signature section, click the **Signature Picker** button.

TIP

You can delete a signature by clicking the name of the signature in the Signature Picker dialog box, clicking the **Remove** button, and clicking **Yes** in the alert box.

The Signature Picker dialog box is displayed.

CLICK: The **New** button.

The Create New Signature dialog box is displayed.

TYPE: **Fun**

CLICK: **Next**

The Edit Signature dialog box appears.

TYPE: **"I'm a great believer in luck, and I find the harder I work, the more I have of it. "**
--Thomas Jefferson

CLICK: **Finish**

CLICK: **OK**

Notice that Fun appears in the Use this signature by default text box. Because this is a signature that you wouldn't use at work, (and you probably use e-mail for work more than you use it for play), you will change the default signature to None.

CLICK: The Use this signature by default drop-down arrow, and click **<None>**.

CLICK: **OK**

2. **Create a message.**

CLICK: The **New Mail Message**  on the toolbar.

TYPE: Your e-mail address.

CLICK: In the Subject text box, and type **Hello**.

PRESS: **Enter**

TYPE: **What are you doing over the weekend?**

PRESS: **Enter** twice.

TYPE: Your name.

PRESS: **Enter** twice.

> Outlook will insert your signature wherever your insertion point is.

3. **Add a signature.**

CLICK: **Insert** on the menu bar.

THEN: Point to **Signature**.

CLICK: **Fun**

> The signature that you created appears, as shown in the figure on the following page.

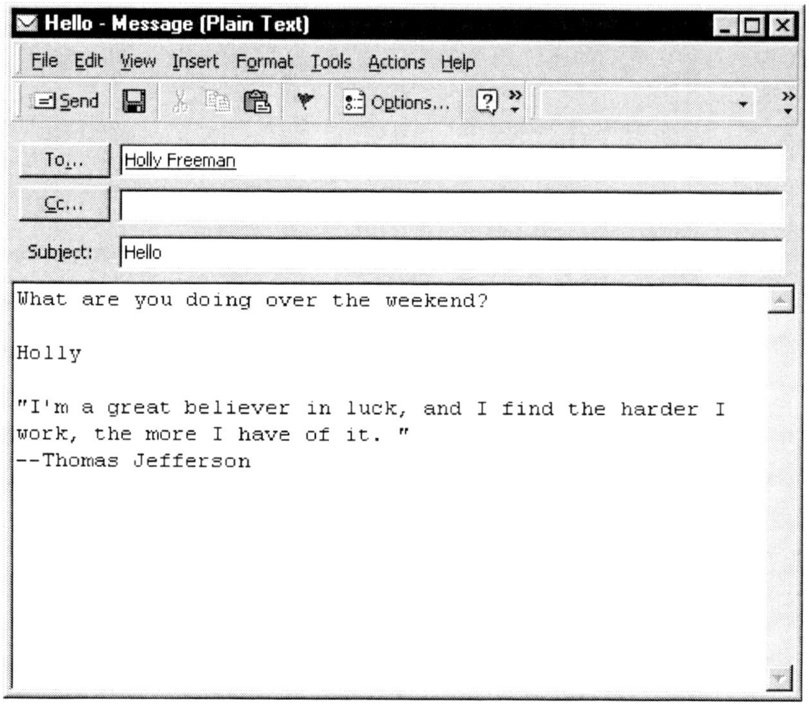

4. **Send the message.**

Adding a vCard to a Message

You can send a vCard of any of your contacts. This comes in handy when someone needs to know the phone number or address of one of your contacts. You simply attach a contact vCard to the message the same way you attach your own vCard to a message.

To attach your vCard to a message:

❶ Display the Contacts folder.

❷ If necessary, add yourself as a contact.

❸ Right-click your contact card.

❹ Click Forward as vCard to display a message window with your vCard attached as shown on the next page.

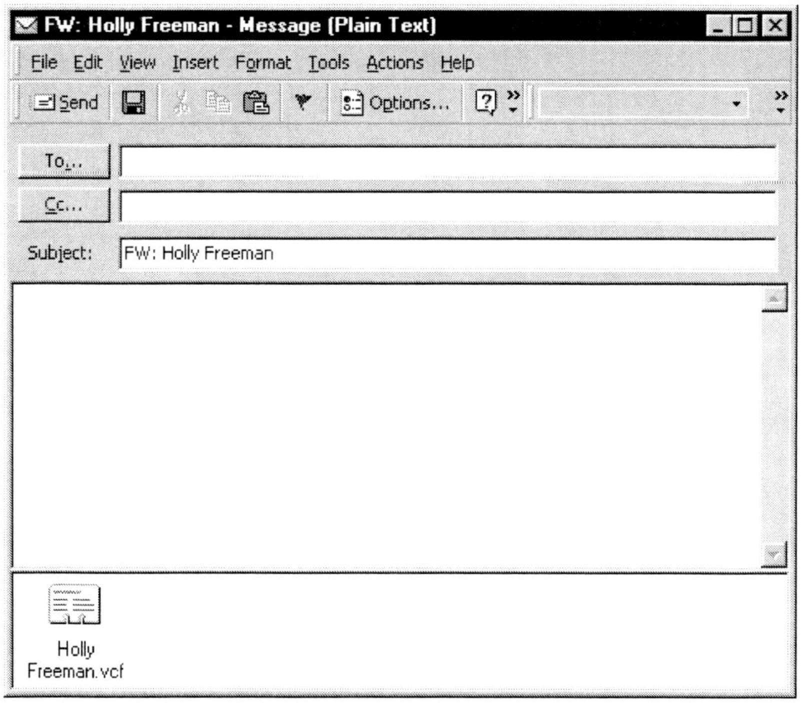

❺ Create and send the message.

If the recipient uses Outlook, he or she can view the vCard by opening it as an attachment. If the recipient uses a different e-mail program the vCard might appear as just text in an e-mail message.

TRY IT 3–6 — ADD A VCARD TO A MESSAGE

In this exercise, you will attach your vCard to an e-mail Message, and send it to yourself.

---

1. **Display the Contacts folder.**
2. **Add yourself as a contact.**
3. **Attach your vCard to an e-mail message.**

   RIGHT-CLICK: Your contact card.

   CLICK: **Forward as vCard**

   A message window appears with your vCard attached. Notice the subject is already filled in.

TYPE: Your e-mail address.

CLICK: In the message list and type **Here's my contact information.**

4. **Send the message.**

5. **Open the vCard.**

FIRST: Display the Inbox.

CLICK: The **Send/Receive** 

button.

The vCard message appears.

DOUBLE-CLICK: The message with the vCard.

The message appears in its own window.

DOUBLE-CLICK: The vCard attachment.

If an alert box appears, click the Open it option and click OK.

TIP

You can click the **Save and Close** button to quickly add the contact information to your Address Book.

6. **Close the contact window and the message window.**

MANAGING E-MAIL ADDRESSES

For Your Information

You can manage your e-mail addresses in many ways. If you use Exchange Server, all users on your network will be listed in the Global Address Book. If you want to create your own list of addresses, you can add entries to Outlook's Personal Address Book. If you want to create an even more specialized list of addresses (whether you use Exchange Server or not) you can create a named group of addresses. Then you can send the group an e-mail message so that each member of the group will receive the message simultaneously. Finally, you can import addresses from Microsoft Access into Outlook.

Creating a Personal Address Book

Because the Outlook Address Book contains e-mail addresses for every user on the network, you probably will not need to use every e-mail address. So you can create a personal address book that will contain only the addresses that you use.

To add a Personal Address Book:

❶ Click Tools on the menu bar.

❷ Click Services on the Tools menu to display the Services dialog box, as shown on the following page.

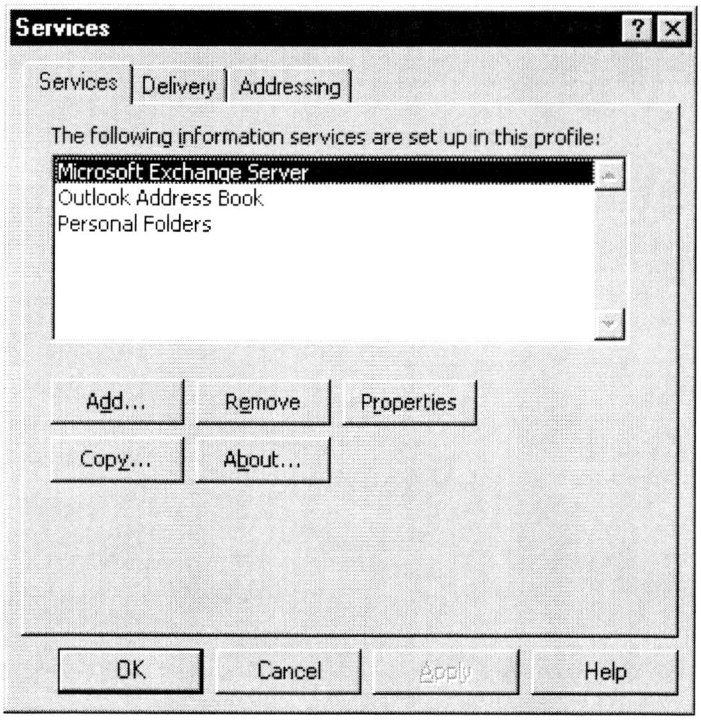

3. Click the Add button to display the Add Service to Profile dialog box.
4. Scroll down and click Personal Address Book.
5. Click OK four times.
6. Restart Outlook.
7. Click Tools on the menu bar.
8. Click Services on the Tools menu.
9. Click the Addressing tab.
10. Click the Add button.
11. Scroll down and click Personal Address Book.
12. Click the Add button.
13. Click the Close button.
14. Click the Keep personal addresses in drop-down arrow, and click Personal Address Book.
15. Click OK.

16. Click the Address Book button on the toolbar.

⓱ Click a contact.

⓲ Click the Add to Personal Address Book button.

To display the Personal Address Book:

❶ Click the Address Book button.

❷ Click the Show Names from the drop-down arrow.

❸ Click Personal Address Book.

TRY IT 3–7 — CREATE A PERSONAL ADDRESS BOOK

In this exercise, you will create a Personal Address book and display it.

---

1. Create a Personal Address book.

CLICK: **Tools** on the menu bar.

CLICK: **Services** on the Tools menu.

The Services dialog box is displayed.

CLICK: The **Add** button.

The Add Service to Profile dialog box is displayed:

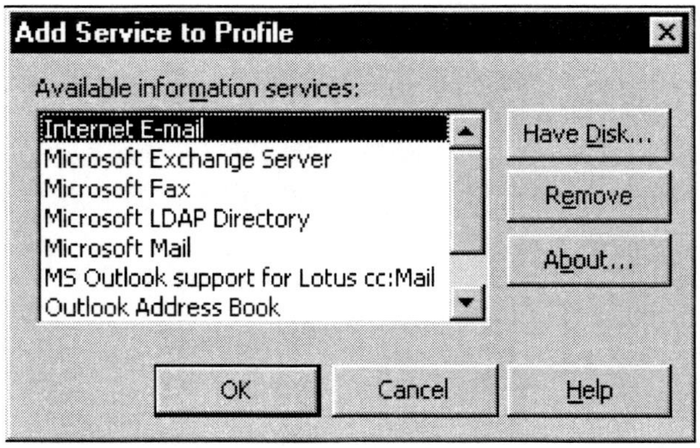

THEN: Scroll down, if necessary, and click **Personal Address Book**.

CLICK: **OK**

The Personal Address Book dialog box appears.

CLICK: **OK**

An alert box appears telling you that you need to restart Outlook.

CLICK: **OK** twice.

THEN: Restart Outlook.

CLICK: **Tools** on the menu bar.

CLICK: **Services** on the Tools menu.

The Services dialog box appears.

CLICK: The **Addressing** tab.

CLICK: The **Add** button.

The Add Address List dialog box appears, as shown below:

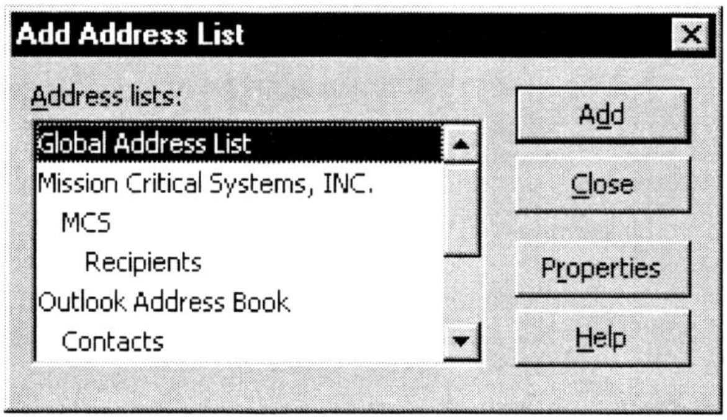

THEN: Scroll down and click **Personal Address Book**.

CLICK: The **Add** button.

CLICK: The **Close** button.

CLICK: The Keep personal addresses in drop-down arrow, and click **Personal Address Book**.

CLICK: **OK**

2. **Add a contact to the Personal Address Book.**

CLICK: The **Address Book** button on the toolbar.

The Address Book appears.

CLICK: Your class partner's name.

CLICK: The **Add to Personal Address Book** button.

Your class partner is now also in the Personal Address Book.

3. **View the Personal Address Book.**

CLICK: The Show Names from the drop-down arrow.

CLICK: **Personal Address Book**

Your class partner is displayed in the Personal Address Book.

CLICK: The **Close** button in the top-right corner of the Address Book.

Creating a Personal Distribution List

A personal distribution list is a collection of contacts who have something in common (such as they all work in a specific department). You use this list to send a message to everyone named in the list. For example, the human resources manager at Lakewood Mountain Resort created a personal distribution list called Marketing Department, so that she could send periodic e-mail messages about departmental meetings to everyone in the marketing department.

To create a personal distribution list:

❶ Click File on the menu bar.

❷ Point to New.

❸ Click Distribution List to display the following window:

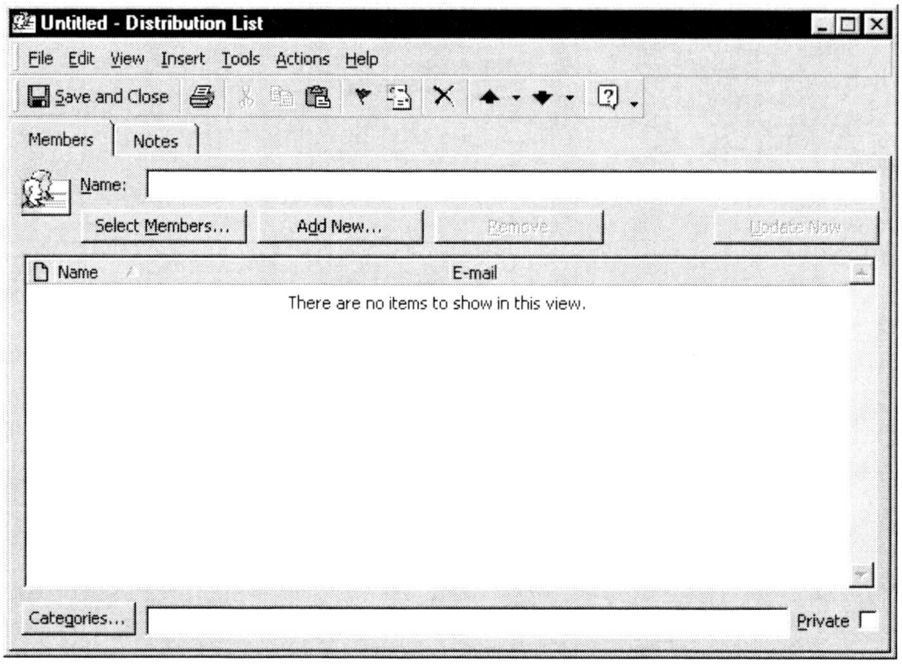

❹ In the Name text box, type a name.

❺ Click the Select Members button to display the Select Members dialog box:

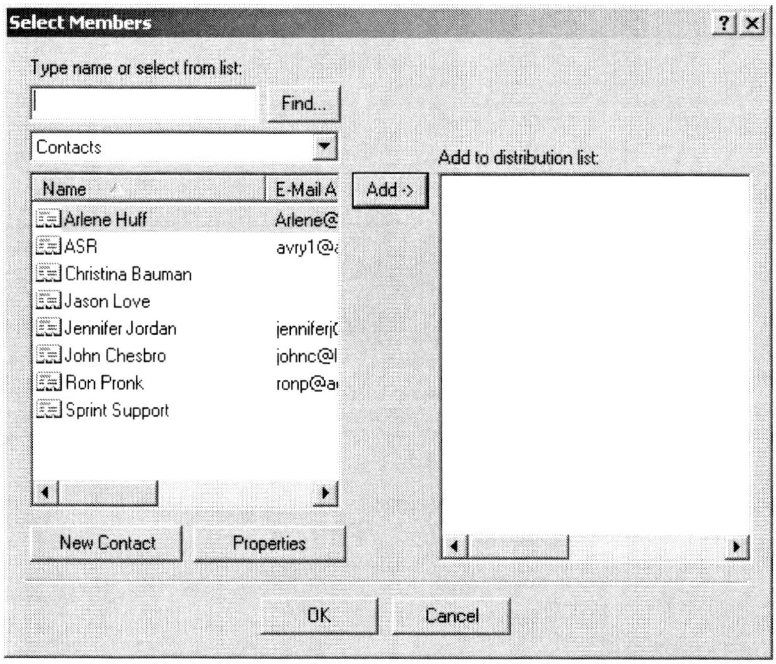

6. Click the name of the contact in the list.

7. Click the Add button.

8. Repeat steps 6 through 7, as necessary.

9. If necessary, click the New Contact button to add a new contact.

10. Click OK.

11. Click the Save and Close button.

TRY IT 3–8 — CREATE A PERSONAL DISTRIBUTION LIST

In this exercise, you will create a personal distribution list called Marketing Department. You will then send a message to the group.

---

1. Create a distribution list.

CLICK: **File** on the menu bar.

THEN: Point to **New**.

CLICK: **Distribution List**

The Distribution List window appears.

THEN: In the Name text box, type **Marketing Department**.

CLICK: The **Select Members** button.

The Select Members dialog box appears.

CLICK: **John Chesbro**

CLICK: The **Add** button.

CLICK: **Ron Pronk**

CLICK: The **Add** button.

TIP

You can select more than one name at a time to add the names to the distribution list. Click the first name of the person you want to add, press **Ctrl**, and then click the rest of the names. When all names are selected, click the **Add** button.

2. **Create two new contacts to add to the list.**

CLICK: The **New Contact** button.

The Properties dialog box appears.

TYPE: **Briggs**

PRESS: **Tab** twice.

TYPE: **Newman**

CLICK: In the E-mail Addresses text box, and type **briggs@lmr.com**.

CLICK: **OK**

Briggs Newman is added to the Name list.

CLICK: The **Add** button.

Briggs Newman is added to the distribution list.

CLICK: The **New Contact** button.

The Properties dialog box appears.

TYPE: **Saul**

PRESS: **Tab** twice.

TYPE: **Forbes**

CLICK: In the E-mail Addresses text box and type **saul@lmr.com**.

CLICK: **OK**

Saul Forbes is added to the Name list.

CLICK: The **Add** button.

Saul Forbes is added to the distribution list.

CLICK: **OK**

The distribution list is completed and should look similar to the figure on the following page.

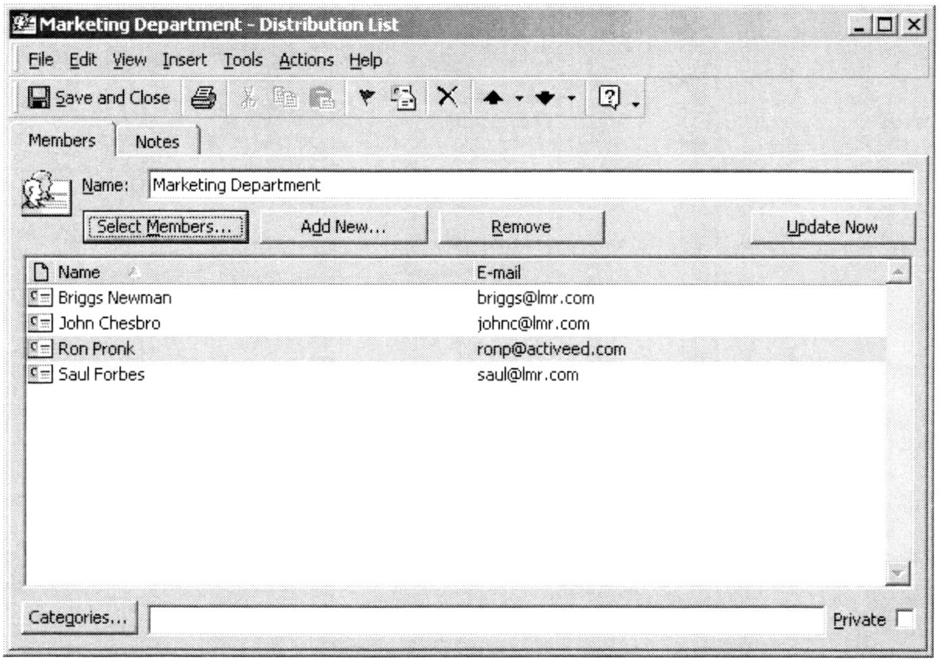

CLICK: The **Save and Close** button.

3. **Display the Inbox.**

4. **Send an e-mail to the marketing department.**

CLICK: The **New Mail Message** 

button.

A message window appears.

CLICK: The **To** button.

The Select names dialog box appears (as shown on the next page). Notice that the Marketing Department distribution list is added to the list and appears with a distribution list icon to the left of it.

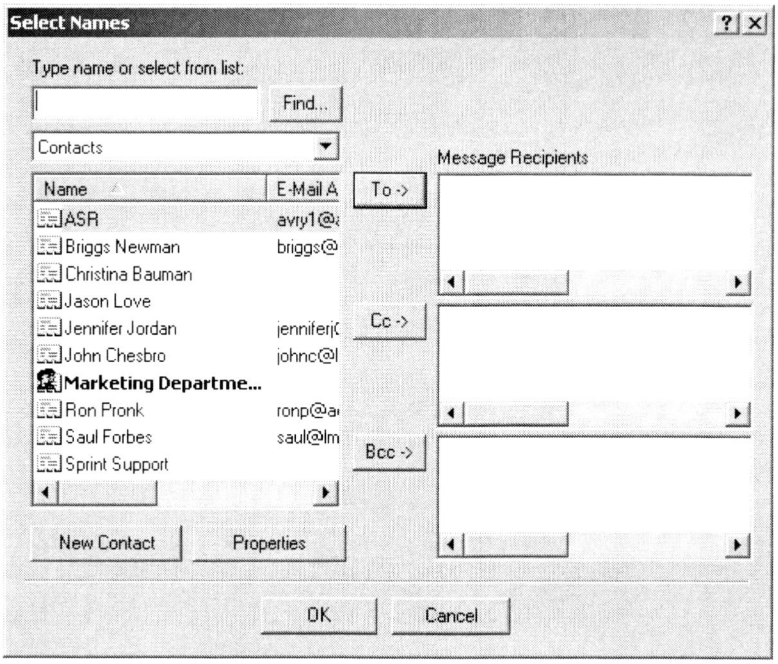

CLICK: **Marketing Department**

CLICK: The **To** button.

CLICK: **OK**

The message window reappears with Marketing Department now in the To text box.

CLICK: In the Subject text box and type **Meeting**.

PRESS: **Enter**

TYPE: **A marketing meeting will be held in the auditorium on Tuesday at 2:00.**

The message is ready to be sent; however, you will not send this message, because the e-mail addresses are fictitious. If the e-mail addresses were real and you sent this message, each person on the distribution list would receive this message.

5. **Close the message without saving changes.**

Importing Addresses from Access into Outlook

The marketing director created a database of contacts in Microsoft Access. She then decided that it would be useful to also have the contacts in Outlook. So she imported the Microsoft Access contact information into Outlook.

If your Access field names (such as First name, Street, or City) are not named exactly the same as the field names in the Contact window (where you add the contact information), don't worry. The Import and Export Wizard has a feature that lets you map your Access field names (which are called values) to the corresponding Outlook field names. Mapping is not a requirement; however, if you choose not to map values to fields, most likely, not all of the information that you typed in Access will appear in Outlook.

To import the Address Book into Microsoft Access:

❶ Click File on the menu bar.

❷ Click Import and Export on the File menu.

❸ Click Next.

❹ Scroll down and click Microsoft Access.

❺ Click Next.

❻ Click the Browse button and navigate to the folder that contains the Access file that you want to import.

❼ Double-click the Access file.

❽ Click Next.

❾ Click the Contacts folder.

❿ Click Next.

⓫ Click the file in the Import a File dialog box.

⓬ Click the Map Custom Fields button to display the Map Custom Fields dialog box, shown in the figure below:

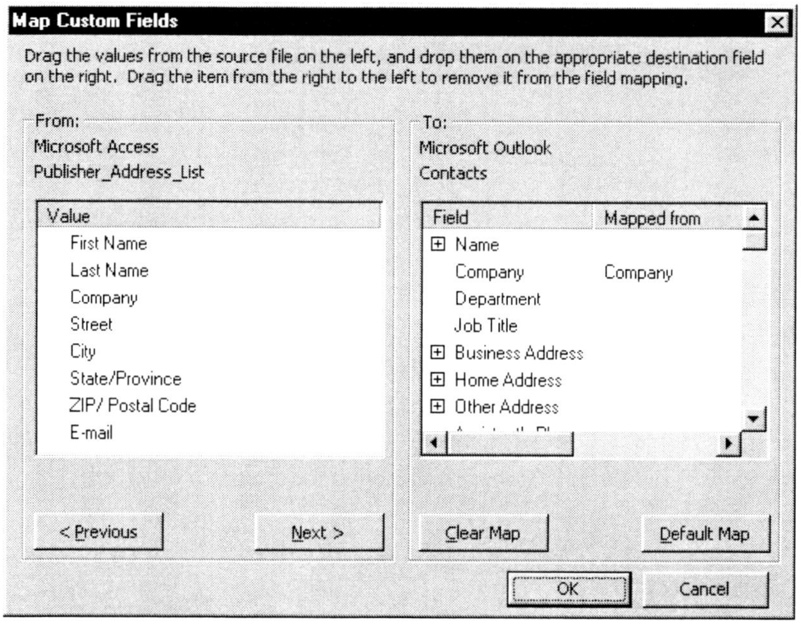

⓭ Drag the field names used in Access onto the corresponding Outlook field names.

⓮ Click OK.

⓯ Click Finish.

> The Small Business Customer Manager dialog box might appear. Click Yes or No each time it appears.

TRY IT 3–9 — IMPORT AN ACCESS DATABASE

In this exercise, you will import a database of addresses from Microsoft Access into the Contacts folder.

---

1. Import a Microsoft Access database into Outlook.

CLICK: **File** on the menu bar.

CLICK: **Import and Export** on the File menu.

> The Import and Export Wizard appears. Import from another program or file is already selected.

CLICK: **Next**

THEN: In the To section, click the plus sign to the left of the Business Address field.

The next wizard dialog box appears.

THEN: Scroll down and click **Microsoft Access**.

CLICK: **Next**

You must have the Import/Export engine feature installed for this exercise to work. If an alert box appears at this point, insert the appropriate CD-ROM to install the feature.

The next wizard dialog box appears.

CLICK: The **Browse** button and navigate to the Outlook Intermediate folder on the exercise diskette.

DOUBLE-CLICK: The Guests file.

CLICK: **Next**

The next wizard dialog box appears.

THEN: If necessary, click the Contacts folder.

CLICK: **Next**

The final wizard dialog box appears.

THEN: Select the Import Publisher_ Address_ List… check box.

2. **Map the Access fields to the Outlook fields.**

CLICK: The **Map Custom Fields** button.

The Map Custom Fields dialog box appears.

THEN: In the To section, click the plus sign next to the Name field.

Notice that the values First Name and Last Name appear under the Mapped from column in the To section. Because the value and the field are already the same, you do not have to drag these values onto the name fields.

NEXT: Scroll down to the Business Address field (so that it appears at the top of the list).

THEN: In the To section, click the plus sign to the left of the Business Address field.

The Business Address field is expanded, showing the elements of the field.

NEXT: In the From section, drag the Street value onto the first Business Street field.

The Street value now appears next to the Business Street field, under the Mapped from column.

THEN: In the From section, drag the City value onto the Business City field in the To section.

The City value now appears next to the Business City field, under the Mapped from column.

NEXT: In the From section, drag the State/Province value onto the Business State field in the To section.

The State/Provence value now appears next to the Business State field, under the Mapped from column.

THEN: In the From section, drag the Zip/Postal Code value onto the Business Post… field in the To section.

The Zip/Postal Code value now appears next to the Business Post… field, under the Mapped from column. Your screen should look similar to the figure on the following page.

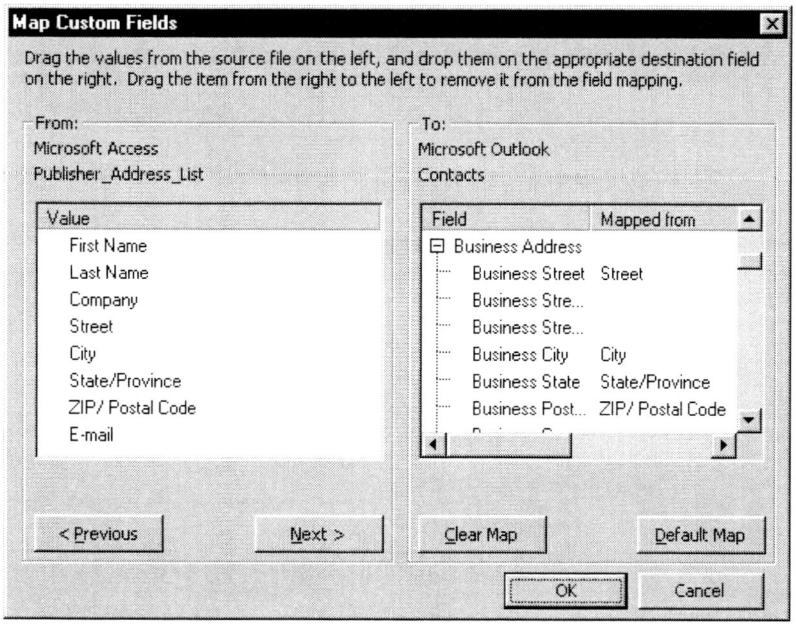

NEXT: Scroll down in the To list until you see the E-mail field.

The e-mail field and the value are the same, so you don't need to drag the value onto the field.

CLICK: **OK**

CLICK: **Finish**

A progress bar appears as the Access files are imported into the Contact folder.

3. Display the Contacts folder to see the new contacts.

USING MAIL TEMPLATES

For Your Information

If you have a certain message that you send over and over again, you can save the message as a template so that it can easily be reused.

Creating Mail Templates

The customer service manager at Lakewood Mountain Resort requires that all of the customer service representatives send a daily e-mail to him about guest complaints, suggestions, and compliments, and how problems, if any, were solved.

To create a mail template:

1. Select or open a message.
2. Click File on the menu bar.
3. Click Save As on the File menu.
4. Click the Save As type drop-down arrow and click Outlook Template.
5. If desired type a name in the File Name text box.
6. Click the Save button.

To use an e-mail template to compose mail:

1. Click File on the menu bar.
2. Point to New on the File menu.
3. Click Choose Form.
4. Click the Look In drop-down arrow.
5. Click User Templates in File System.
6. Click the name of the template.
7. Click Open.

❽ Make any necessary changes.

❾ Send the message.

Using the Clipboard to Create a Template

If you're familiar with Microsoft Word, you've probably used the *Clipboard*. The Clipboard is an area in your computer's memory that Windows reserves to temporarily store content when you cut or copy text and graphics.

You could use the Clipboard to help you create a mail template. Simply copy useful text from an old e-mail message (which will put it on the Clipboard) and paste it into the template.

To use the Clipboard for an e-mail template:

❶ Select the text you want to copy.

❷ Right-click the text.

❸ Click Copy.

❹ Display the e-mail template.

❺ Right-click the location where you want the text.

❻ Click Paste.

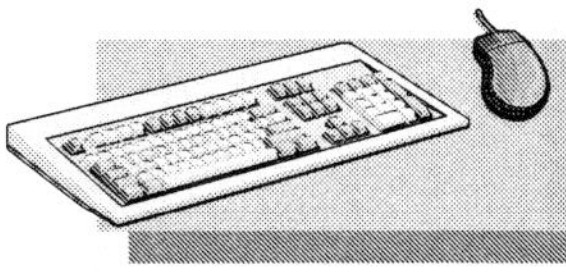

TRY IT 3–10 — CREATE A MAIL TEMPLATE

In this exercise, you will create a message, cut text from an old e-mail message, and paste it into the message you just created, then save the message as a template. Finally, you will use the template to send an e-mail message.

---

1. Create a message.

FIRST: Display the Inbox.

CLICK: The **New Mail Message** [New] button on the toolbar.

A message window appears.

TYPE: Your e-mail address.

CLICK: In the Subject text box.

TYPE: **Update**

PRESS: **Enter**

CLICK: In the message box.

TYPE: **Customer Complaints:**

PRESS: **Enter** four times.

TYPE: **Customer Suggestions:**

PRESS: **Enter** four times.

TYPE: **Customer Compliments:**

PRESS: **Enter** four times.

TYPE: **Solved Problems:**

2. **Copy text from an existing e-mail to add to the template.**

CLICK: The **Inbox** button on the taskbar.

DOUBLE-CLICK: The message that has the subject Marketing Update.

NEXT: Select the text *Lakewood Mountain Resort Daily Update:*

RIGHT-CLICK: The text.

CLICK: **Copy**

CLICK: The **Close** button in the top-right corner of the message window.

CLICK: The **Update** button on the taskbar to display the mail template that you are in the process of creating.

NEXT: Position the insertion point before the text Customer Complaints.

PRESS: **Enter** twice, and position the insertion point at the top of the message box.

RIGHT-CLICK: The blank line.

CLICK: **Paste**

TIP

You can add the Clipboard toolbar to a message window. Right-click a toolbar and click **Clipboard**. You use this toolbar to paste multiple items that you copied from any Microsoft Office application.

The text you copied from another e-mail message is pasted into the current message.

3. **Save the message as a mail template.**

CLICK: **File** on the menu bar.

CLICK: **Save As** on the File menu.

The Save As dialog box appears.

CLICK: The Save as type drop-down arrow.

CLICK: **Outlook Template**

CLICK: The **Save** button.

The message is now a template. Your template should look similar to the following:

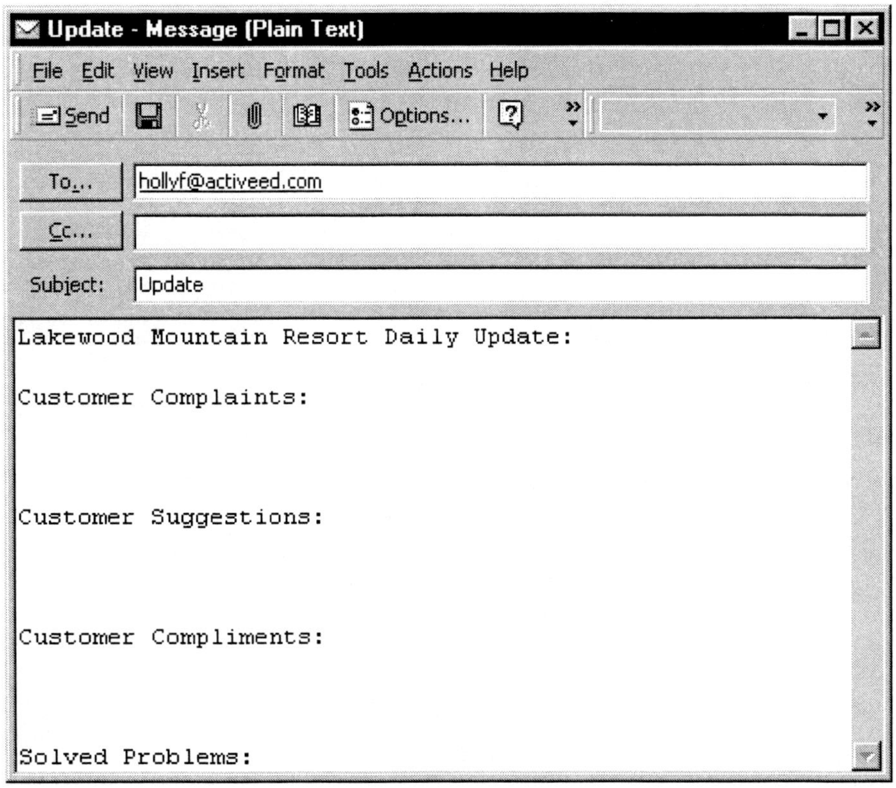

CLICK: The **Close** button in the top-right corner of the template.

CLICK: **Yes** in the alert box that appears.

The template is saved and closed.

4. Use the template to compose mail.

CLICK: **File** on the menu bar.

THEN: Point to **New** on the File menu.

CLICK: **Choose Form**

The Choose Form dialog box appears as shown below:

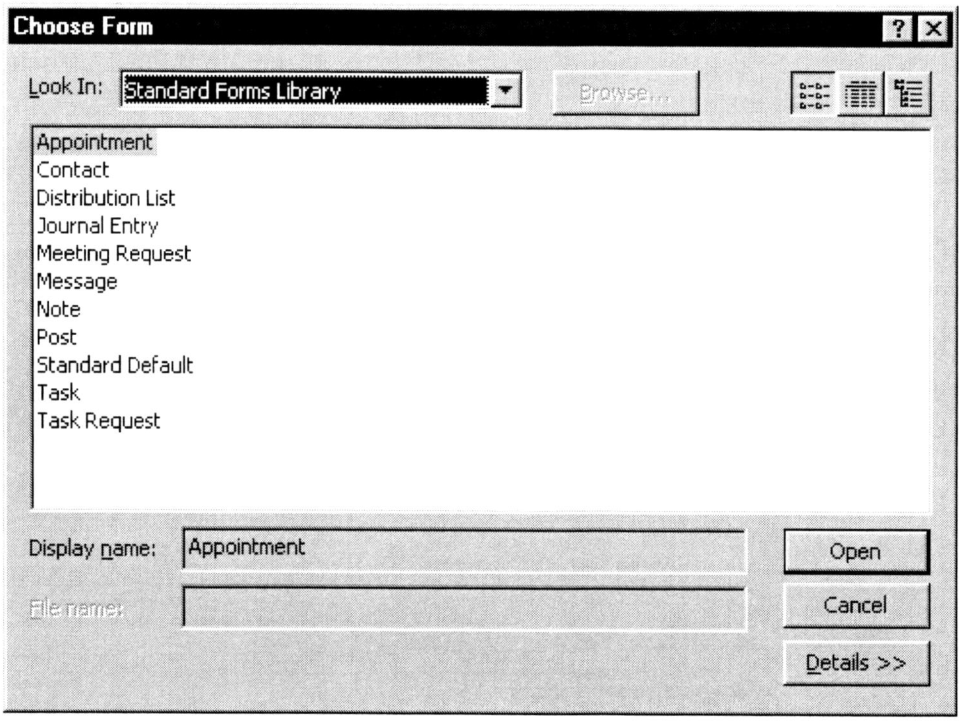

CLICK: The Look In drop-down arrow and click **User Templates in File System**.

The name of the template you created appears.

CLICK: **Update**

CLICK: **Open**

The template appears.

THEN: Position the insertion point on the second blank line after the text Customer Complaints.

TYPE: **None**

NEXT: Position the insertion point on the second blank line after the text Customer Suggestions.

TYPE: **Customer wants magazines by the hot tub.**

THEN: Position the insertion point on the second blank line after the text Customer Compliments.

TYPE: **Lmr is in a beautiful location!**

NEXT: Position the insertion point after the text Solved Problems and press Enter twice.

TYPE: **Put magazines by the hot tub.**

The e-mail message should look similar to the following:

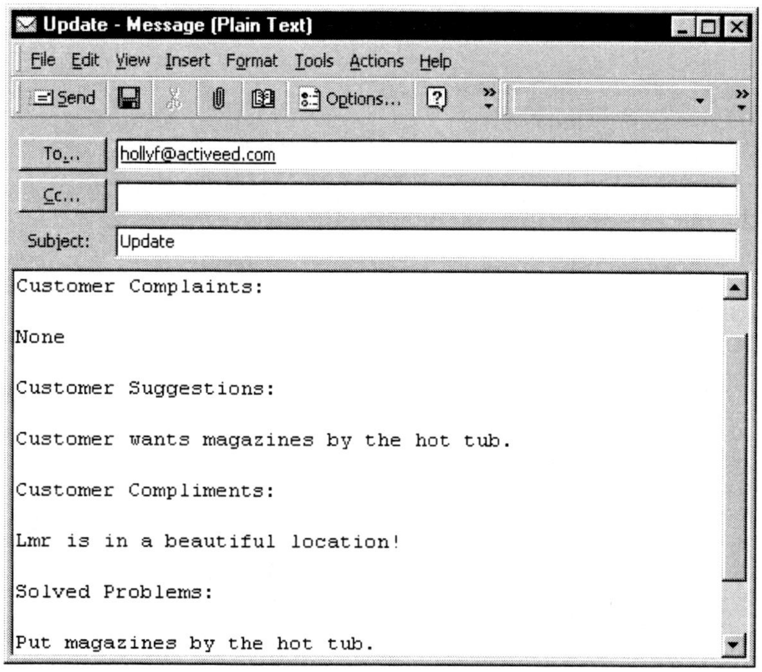

THEN: Send the message.

QuickLook at Lesson 3

To	Do This
Use the Rules Wizard	**1.** Display the Inbox. **2.** Click **Tools** on the menu bar. **3.** Click **Rules Wizard** on the Tools menu. **4.** Click the **New** button to display the Rules Wizard. **5.** Follow the Rules Wizard instructions, clicking **Next** after completing each dialog box. **6.** When you are finished specifying options, click **Finish**.
Sort mail messages	**1.** Click the column heading that you want to sort by to toggle between ascending and descending order.
Track mail messages	**1.** Create a message, then click the **Options** button in the message window to display the Message Options dialog box. **2.** In the Tracking options section, select the Request a read receipt for this message check box. **3.** Click the **Close** button. **4.** Send the message.
View information about AutoArchive	**1.** Click **Tools** on the menu bar. **2.** Click **Options** on the Tools menu. **3.** Click the **Other** tab. **4.** Click the **AutoArchive** button to display the AutoArchive dialog box. *Or* **1.** Display the Folder List. **2.** Right-click the Inbox folder. **3.** Click **Properties**. **4.** Click the **AutoArchive** tab. *Or* **1.** Click **File** on the menu bar. **2.** Click **Archive** on the File menu to display the Archive dialog box.

To	Do This
Manually archive mail messages	**1.** Click **File** on the menu bar. **2.** Click **Archive** on the File menu. **3.** If necessary, click the **Archive this folder and all subfolders** button. **4.** Click a folder. **5.** Click the Archive items older than drop-down arrow and select a date. **6.** Click **OK**.
Restore an archive file	**1.** Click **File** on the menu bar. **2.** Click **Import and Export** on the File menu. **3.** Click **Next**. **4.** Scroll down and click **Personal Folder File (.pst)**. **5.** Click **Next**. **6.** If necessary, navigate to where your archive file is stored. **7.** Click **Next**. **8.** Click the appropriate import options. **9.** Click **Finish**.
Create a signature	**1.** Click **Tools** on the menu bar. **2.** Click **Options** on the Tools menu. **3.** Click the **Mail Format** tab. **4.** In the Signature section, click the **Signature Picker** button to display the Signature Picker dialog box. **5.** Click the **New** button to display the Create New Signature dialog box. **6.** Type a name for the signature. **7.** Click **Next** to display the Edit Signature dialog box. **8.** Type the text of the signature. **9.** Click **Finish**. **10.** Click **OK** twice.
Add a signature to a message that doesn't already have one	**1.** Create a message. **2.** In the message window, click **Insert** on the menu bar. **3.** Point to **Signature**. **4.** Click the signature that you want to use.

To	Do This
Attach your vCard to a message	**1.** Display the Contacts folder. **2.** If necessary, add yourself as a contact. **3.** Right-click your contact card. **4.** Click **Forward as vCard** to display a message window with your vCard attached. **5.** Create and send the message.
Add a Personal Address Book	**1.** Click **Tools** on the menu bar. **2.** Click **Services** on the Tools menu to display the Services dialog box. **3.** Click the **Add** button to display the Add Service to Profile dialog box. **4.** Scroll down, and click **Personal Address Book**. **5.** Click **OK** four times. **6.** Restart Outlook. **7.** Click **Tools** on the menu bar. **8.** Click **Services** on the Tools menu. **9.** Click the **Addressing** tab. **10.** Click the **Add** button. **11.** Scroll down, and click **Personal Address Book**. **12.** Click the **Add** button. **13.** Click the **Close** button. **14.** Click the Keep personal addresses in drop-down arrow, and click **Personal Address Book**. **15.** Click **OK**. **16.** Click the **Address Book** button on the toolbar. **17.** Click a contact. **18.** Click the **Add to Personal Address Book** button.
Display the Personal Address Book	**1.** Click the **Address Book** button. **2.** Click the Show Names from the drop-down arrow. **3.** Click **Personal Address Book**.

To	Do This
Create a personal distribution list	**1.** Click **File** on the menu bar. **2.** Point to **New**. **3.** Click **Distribution List**. **4.** In the Name text box, type a name. **5.** Click the **Select Members** button to display the Select Members dialog box. **6.** Click the name of the contact in the list. **7.** Click the **Add** button. **8.** Repeat steps 6 through 7 as necessary. **9.** If necessary, click the **New Contact** button to add a new contact. **10.** Click **OK**. **11.** Click the **Save and Close** button.
Import the Address Book into Microsoft Access	**1.** Click **File** on the menu bar. **2.** Click **Import and Export** on the File menu. **3.** Click **Next**. **4.** Scroll down, and click **Microsoft Access**. **5.** Click **Next**. **6.** Click the **Browse** button and navigate to the folder that contains the Access file that you want to import. **7.** Double-click the Access file. **8.** Click **Next**. **9.** Click the **Contacts** folder. **10.** Click **Next**. **11.** Click the file in the Import a File dialog box. **12.** Click the **Map Custom Fields** button to display the Map Custom Fields dialog box. **13.** Drag the field names used in Access onto the corresponding Outlook field names. **14.** Click **OK**. **15.** Click **Finish**.
Create a mail template	**1.** Select or open a message. **2.** Click **File** on the menu bar. **3.** Click **Save As** on the File menu. **4.** Click the Save As type drop-down arrow, and click **Outlook Template**. **5.** If desired type a name in the File Name text box. **6.** Click the **Save** button.

To	Do This
Use an e-mail template to compose mail	**1.** Click **File** on the menu bar. **2.** Point to **New** on the File menu. **3.** Click **Choose Form**. **4.** Click the Look in drop-down arrow. **5.** Click **User Templates in File System**. **6.** Click the name of the template. **7.** Click **Open**. **8.** Make any necessary changes. **9.** Send the message.
Use the Clipboard for an e-mail template	**1.** Select the text you want to copy. **2.** Right-click the text. **3.** Click **Copy**. **4.** Display the e-mail template. **5.** Right-click the location where you want the text. **6.** Click **Paste**.

SkillCheck – Lesson 3

1. Create a Rule called Attachments that states messages that you receive that have an attachment will be copied to a folder called Attachments.

2. Sort messages by icon.

3. Send a message to your class partner about going to a seminar, and request a read receipt.

4. View information about AutoArchive using the AutoArchive dialog box.

5. Create a signature called Nickname that will automatically add your nickname to every e-mail message that you create. (If you don't have one, create one.)

6. Attach a vCard for Ron Pronk to an e-mail message to your class partner.

7. Add a contact named Shirley Forlorn with the e-mail address Shirley@frown.com to your Personal Address Book.

8. Create a personal distribution list called Clients. Add the following contacts to the list: Byron Plummer, Chris Leigh, Herb Anderson, and Kate Cadrow.

9. Import the Microsoft Access file called LMR Address List (on the exercise diskette) to the Contacts folder.

10. Create a mail template called Weekly Repairs Report. Use the following information to create the template:

Date:
Description and Cost of Each Repair:
Total Cost:
Damages Caused By:

11. Use the Weekly Repairs Report template to send a message to your class partner.

Answers to the SkillChecks can be found here: **http://www.activeed.com/skanswers/outlook2.htm**

Performance Objectives

You will learn how to:

- Configure Calendar options
- Schedule events and meetings
- Use the Calendar on the Web
- Share Calendar information over the Web

CONFIGURING CALENDAR OPTIONS

For Your Information

The Calendar, by default, displays a Monday through Friday, 8:00 A.M. to 5:00 P.M. work week. This work week might not come close to fitting your work schedule. For example, your work week might start on a Tuesday and end on Saturday. Also, the Calendar doesn't automatically show holidays from different countries, different time zones, or the numbers of the weeks (1 through 52). These might be options that you need, or would like to have. For that reason, Outlook lets you customize the Calendar to fit your needs.

Modifying the Calendar

The following table details some of the Calendar options you can configure using the Calendar Options dialog box.

Calendar Option	What It Does
Sun, Mon, Tue, Wed, Thu, Fri, Sat check boxes	Depending on which check boxes you select, displays only those days as working days in 5 work week view. This is useful if the days that you work are non-traditional.
First day of week	Arranges the Calendar so that specified day is the first day of the work week.
First week of year	Specifies whether you want the first week of the year to start on January 1, the first 4-day week, or the first full week.
Start time	Specifies what time you begin your workday.
End time	Specifies what time you end your workday.
Show week numbers in the Date Navigator	Displays the numbers of the weeks of the year from 1 to 52 to the left of each week in the Date Navigator.

Calendar Option	What It Does
Always use local Calendar	Lets you work from a copy of your calendar on your local computer instead of on the server.
Background color	Changes the background color.
Time Zone	Displays a time zone from a country you specify.
Add Holidays	Display holidays from a country you specify.
Free/Busy Options	Lets other people know when you are available for meetings. Also lets you set how much information you want to share.

You can customize the appearance of the menus and toolbars in the Calendar by right-clicking a toolbar or menu name, and clicking Customize (the Customize dialog box will appear). On the Toolbars tab, you can add or remove toolbars. On the Commands tab, you can click a category in the Categories list, and drag a command onto a toolbar or menu. Conversely, you can drag a command off of the toolbar or menu when the Customize dialog box is displayed. Finally, on the Options tab, you can click the Reset my usage data button to restore the toolbar and menus to their default settings. You can also display the toolbar buttons with large icons, turn off the options to list font names in their font, show ScreenTips on toolbars, show shortcut keys in ScreenTips, and turn on various menu animations.

To configure Calendar options:

❶ Click Tools on the menu bar.

❷ Click Options on the Tools menu.

You must set your E-mail Services options to Corporate or Workgroup to configure Calendar options. (Display your Inbox, click Tools, click Options, click the Mail Delivery tab, and click the Reconfigure Mail Support button. In the dialog box click the Corporate or Workgroup option, click the Next button, and then follow the screen prompts.)

❸ Click the Calendar Options button to display the Calendar Options dialog box, shown on the following page.

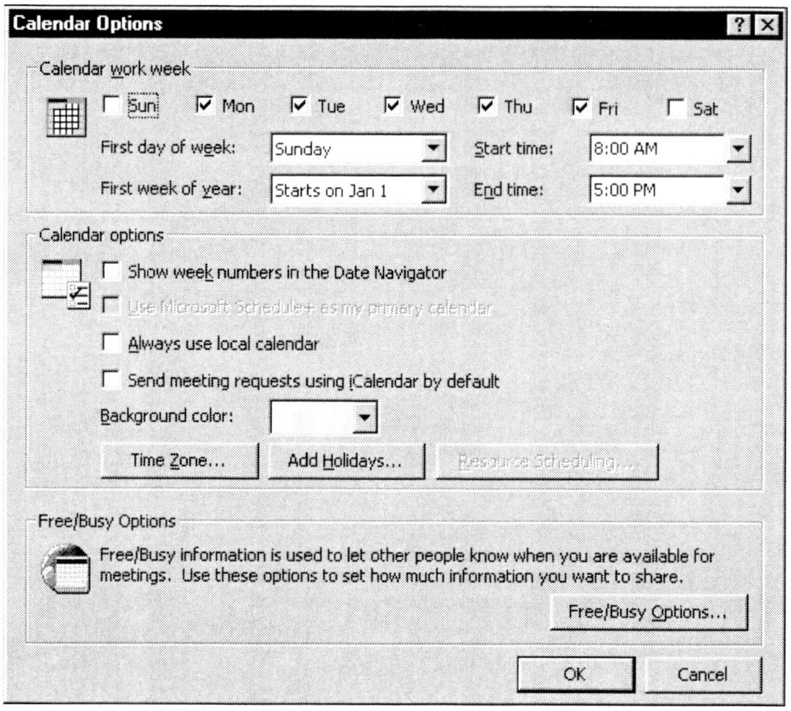

❹ Change options as desired.

❺ Click OK twice.

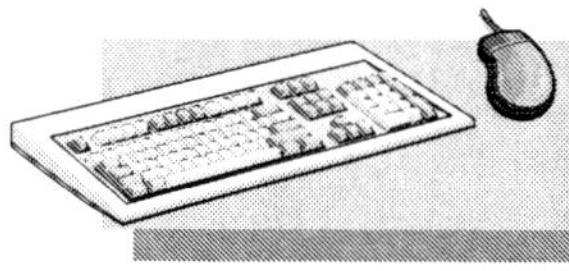

TRY IT 4–1 — CHANGE CALENDAR OPTIONS

In this exercise, you will create a work week that starts on Wednesday and ends on Sunday. You will also set the job's starting time to 2:00 P.M., and the ending time to 10:00 P.M. You will then change the Calendar's background color. Finally, you will configure Outlook to show holdiays from the United Kingdom.

---

1. **Display the Calendar.**
2. **Display the Calendar in Work Week view.**

   CLICK: The **Work Week** [5 Work Week] button on the toolbar.

   The Calendar is displayed in Work Week view. Notice that the default work week is Monday through Friday, 8:00 A.M. to 5:00 P.M.

3. **Create a custom work week.**

CLICK: **Tools** on the menu bar.

CLICK: **Options** on the Tools menu.

The Options dialog box appears.

CLICK: The **Calendar Options** button.

The Calendar Options dialog box appears.

THEN: Select the Sun check box, clear the Mon and Tue check boxes, and then select the Sat check box.

The days that you want to display as work days are selected.

CLICK: The First day of the week drop-down arrow, and click **Wednesday**.

Wednesday is now specified as the first day of the work week.

CLICK: The Start time drop-down arrow, scroll down, and click **2:00 P.M.**

CLICK: The End time drop-down arrow, scroll down, and click **10:00 P.M.**

The starting and ending time of a job is specified.

4. **Change the background color.**

CLICK: The Background Color drop-down arrow.

CLICK: A color that appeals to you.

The background of the Calendar will now be a different color.

5. **Set Outlook to display holidays.**

CLICK: The **Add Holidays** button.

The Add Holidays to Calendar dialog box appears as shown below:

TIP

You can select as many countries as you want.

CLICK: **United Kingdom**

CLICK: **OK**

A progress bar appears as the holidays from the United Kingdom are added to the Calendar.

If an alert box appears, stating that the United States Holidays are already installed on your computer, click No.

CLICK: **OK** twice.

The new options that you specified are activated. Notice that the Calendar now has a new background color, and that the days Wednesday through Sunday are displayed.

6. **Verify that the holiday option is set.**

CLICK: The **Day** [1 Day] button on the toolbar.

The Calendar is displayed in Day view.

THEN: Using either the left or right arrows on the Date Navigator, display the day May 1, 2000.

The Calendar displays the United Kingdom's Bank Holiday.

THEN: Display the current day.

Scheduling Events and Meetings

For Your Information

Outlook lets you schedule various types of activities. You probably already know that in the Calendar, an *appointment* is an activity that you schedule for yourself; you don't need to involve others or reserve resources, such as a conference room. If you want to invite others to or reserve resources for an appointment, you must schedule a *meeting*. You can also schedule an *event*. An event is an activity that has a 24 hour or longer duration. For example, a seminar or a trade show could be considered an event.

Scheduling a Meeting

2000 New!

Outlook 2000 now provides this easier way to schedule a meeting.

To create a meeting, you must invite people. After you select prospective attendees, you then send out an invitation (as shown below), which tells people what the meeting's about, and where and when the meeting will take place.

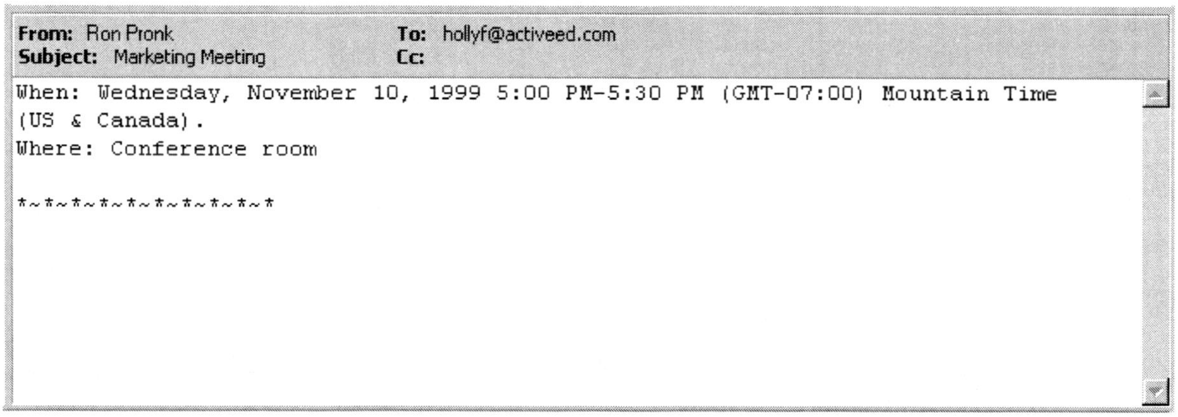
From: Ron Pronk **To:** hollyf@activeed.com
Subject: Marketing Meeting **Cc:**

When: Wednesday, November 10, 1999 5:00 PM-5:30 PM (GMT-07:00) Mountain Time (US & Canada).
Where: Conference room

~~*~*~*~*~*~*~*~*

Some companies have only one or two conference rooms, so often, employees have to schedule a time to use the conference room. In Outlook, the conference room (as well as other office items, such as a slide projector) is considered to be a resource. You can set up a resource, view the resource's availability, and schedule a time to use it.

To set up a resource, click Tools on the menu bar, click Options on the Tools menu, and then click the Calendar Options button. Click Resource Scheduling, and click the desired options.

After a resource is set up, you can schedule a time to use it by clicking Actions on the menu bar, clicking Plan a Meeting on the Actions menu, and clicking the Invite Others button. In the Type Name or Select from List text box, type the name of the resource you want to use for the meeting, click the Resources button, and click OK.

To schedule a meeting:

❶ In the Calendar, display the day that you want to schedule a meeting.

❷ Click the drop-down arrow to the right of the New Appointment button on the toolbar.

❸ Click Meeting Request to display the Meeting window as shown below:

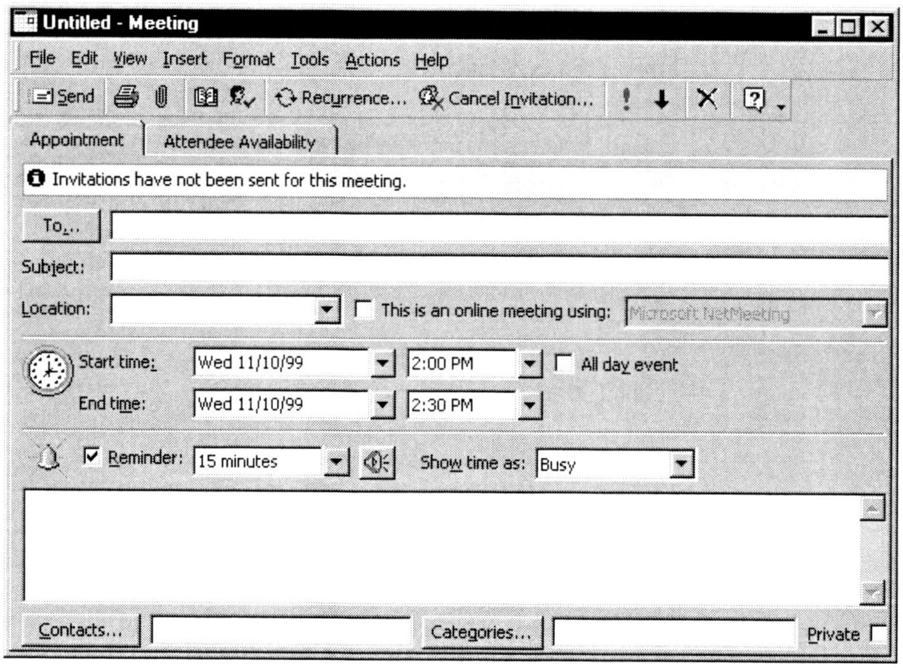

> If you work on Exchange Server, you can click the Attendee Availability tab to select a contact on your network and view whether the contact is available for the time that you want to schedule the meeting.

❹ Click the To button.

❺ Choose prospective attendees by clicking a contact or clicking a group, clicking either the Required or Optional buttons, and clicking OK.

❻ Click in the Subject text box, and type a subject.

❼ Click in the Location text box, and type the location where the meeting will be held.

❽ Modify the Start time and End time options as desired.

❾ Click the Send button.

TRY IT 4–2 — SCHEDULE A MEETING

In this exercise, you will schedule a marketing meeting. You will then send a meeting request to two people in your class.

---

1. **Add a person other than your class partner to your Contacts folder.**
2. **In the Calendar, display next Wednesday.**
3. **Schedule a meeting.**

CLICK: The 4:00 P.M. line in the Calendar.

CLICK: The drop-down arrow to the right of the New Appointment button on the toolbar.

CLICK: **Meeting Request**

The Meeting window is displayed.

CLICK: The **To** button.

The Select Attendees and Resources dialog box appears.

THEN: If necessary, scroll and click your class partner's name.

TIP

You can use the Attendee Availability tab in the Appointment window to choose people to go to the meeting, and to see which people on the network are available to go to the meeting.

CLICK: The **Required** button.

THEN: If necessary, scroll and click the name of the person in your class you just added to the Contacts folder.

CLICK: The **Required** button.

CLICK: **OK**

The meeting request is going to be sent to the people in your class.

CLICK: In the Subject text box, and type **Marketing Meeting**.

CLICK: In the Location text box, and type **Conference Room**.

CLICK: The second End time drop-down arrow and click **5:00 P.M. (1 hour)**.

CLICK: The **Send** Send button.

The meeting requests are sent to the people in your class. The meeting is displayed in your Calendar.

If you are set up for Corporate or Work Group, after you send out a meeting request, the recipient can right-click the request in the Inbox and click Accept, Tentative, or Decline. The meeting organizer can then see who has responded to the meeting by double-clicking the meeting in the Calendar, clicking the Attendee Availability tab, and clicking the Show attendee status option.

Scheduling Real-Time Meetings

You can also schedule a real-time meeting for participants you know will not be able to physically attend. To conduct such a meeting, you can use *Windows NetMeeting*. NetMeeting is an add-on program that enables you to conduct meetings over the Internet. You can communicate to meeting participants by using sound and video. To communicate in this way, you must have a sound card, speakers, a microphone, and video camera installed on your computer. If you do not have the following items, you can still exchange information by typing messages in a Chat window, by drawing on the *Whiteboard* (a blank screen that simulates marker boards used in classrooms or conference rooms), or by sharing files and applications.

The marketing director at Lakewood Mountain Resort wanted a client in Ireland to attend a conference about how the resort is environmentally conscious. Knowing that the client would not be able to fly to Colorado to attend the conference, he invited the client to attend the conference through NetMeeting.

To schedule real-time meetings:

❶ In the Calendar, display the day that you want to schedule a NetMeeting.

❷ Click the drop-down arrow to the right of the New Appointment button on the toolbar.

❸ Click Meeting Request.

❹ Click the To button.

❺ Choose prospective attendees by clicking a contact or clicking a group, clicking either the Required or Optional buttons, and clicking OK.

❻ Click in the Subject text box and type a subject.

❼ Select the This is an online meeting using check box.

❽ If necessary click the This is an online meeting using drop-down arrow, and click Windows NetMeeting.

❾ Modify options as desired.

❿ Click the Send button.

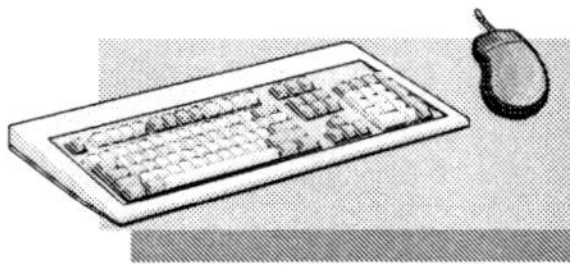

TRY IT 4–3 — SCHEDULE REAL-TIME MEETINGS

In this exercise, you will schedule a NetMeeting with your class partner.

---

1. In the Calendar, display next Thursday.

2. Schedule a NetMeeting.

CLICK: The 5:00 P.M. line in the Calendar.

CLICK: The drop-down arrow to the right of the New Appointment button on the toolbar.

CLICK: **Meeting Request**

The Meeting window is displayed.

CLICK: The **To** button.

The Select Attendees and Resources dialog box appears.

THEN: If necessary, scroll and click your class partner's name.

CLICK: The **Required** button.

CLICK: **OK**

The meeting request is going to be sent your class partner.

CLICK: In the Subject text box, and type **Environmental NetMeeting**.

THEN: Select the This is an online meeting using check box.

The meeting window expands, showing more options (as shown on the next page). Notice that Windows NetMeeting already appears in the This is an online meeting using text box.

TIP

You can schedule a meeting or an appointment to watch a broadcast by clicking the This is an online meeting using the drop-down arrow, and clicking **NetShow Services**. Then, in the Event Address text box, type a Web site that is showing the broadcast.

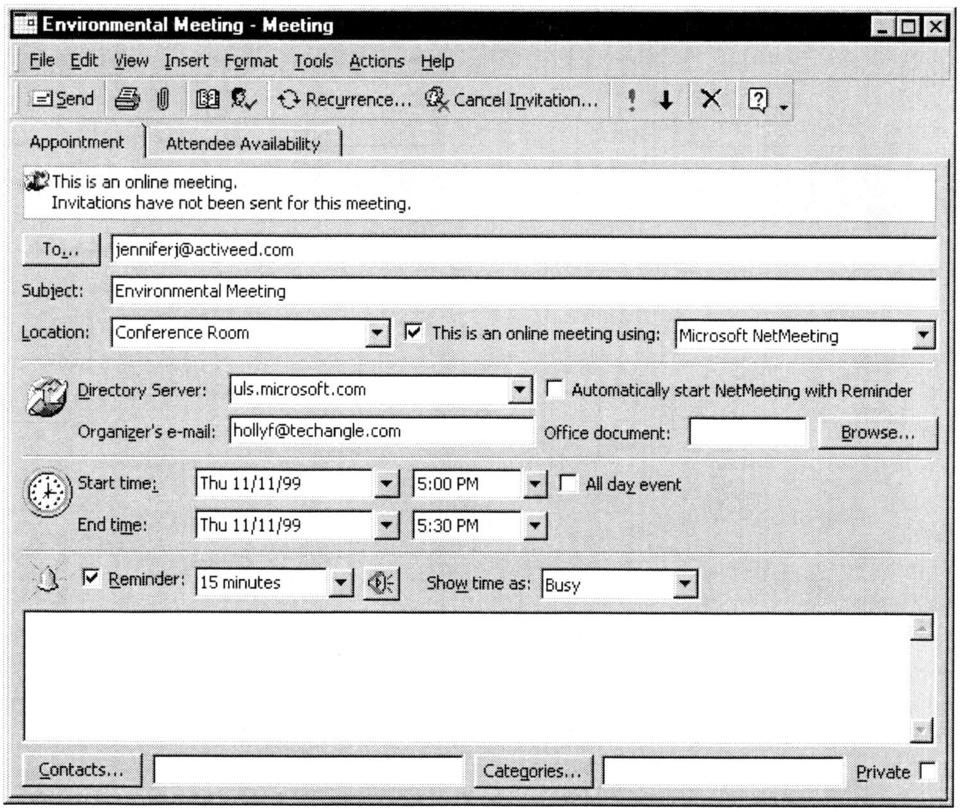

TIP

If you select the Reminder check box and the Automatically start NetMeeting with Reminder check box, Outlook will remind you and the attendee(s) that you have fifteen minutes (or any other time you specify) before NetMeeting will automatically start.

CLICK: The second End time drop-down arrow and click **7:00 P.M. (2 hours)**.

CLICK: The **Send**  button.

The NetMeeting request is sent to your class partner. The meeting is displayed in your Calendar.

To actually participate in a NetMeeting, you must first start NetMeeting, and set up NetMeeting by entering your personal information in the Windows NetMeeting dialog box. You start NetMeeting by right-clicking a real-time meeting in the Calendar. (If you don't have a real-time meeting in the Calendar, you can access NetMeeting by starting Internet Explorer 5, clicking File on the menu bar, pointing to New, and clicking Internet Call.)

You can use an ILS (Internet Locator Service) directory to start a NetMeeting (an ILS directory lists users who are currently connected to a particular computer that serves as a contact point for NetMeeting participants) or you use an IP address to start a NetMeeting. (An IP address uses numbers and dots to identify your computer on the network. You must know both your IP address and a meeting participant's IP address.)

If you want to use a ILS directory, you can start a NetMeeting using the following steps: If necessary, log onto ils.microsoft.com (in NetMeeting, click Call on the menu bar, click Log On to ils.microsoft.com). Then click Call on the menu bar, click Directory, click the person you're calling in the list, and click the Call button.

If you want to use a IP address, you can start a NetMeeting using the following steps: Exchange IP address information with your contact. (To find your IP address, start NetMeeting, click Help on the menu bar, and click About Windows NetMeeting. Your IP Address will be listed at the bottom of the About Windows NetMeeting dialog box after the text IP Addresses.) Type your contact's IP address in the Address text box, and click the Place Call button. (Your contact will have to answer the call.)

To find out more information about how to use NetMeeting, ask your instructor, or visit the NetMeeting Help system.

Scheduling Multi-Day Events

When you schedule a multi-day event, such as a vacation, a trade show, or a seminar, the Calendar displays the event in a banner under the Calendar's date (as shown below). However, the Calendar does not occupy blocks of time like it does when you schedule an appointment or meeting. When viewed by others on a network, an event will be displayed as free, unless you specify that you want the event to be displayed as Tentative, Busy, or Out of Office.

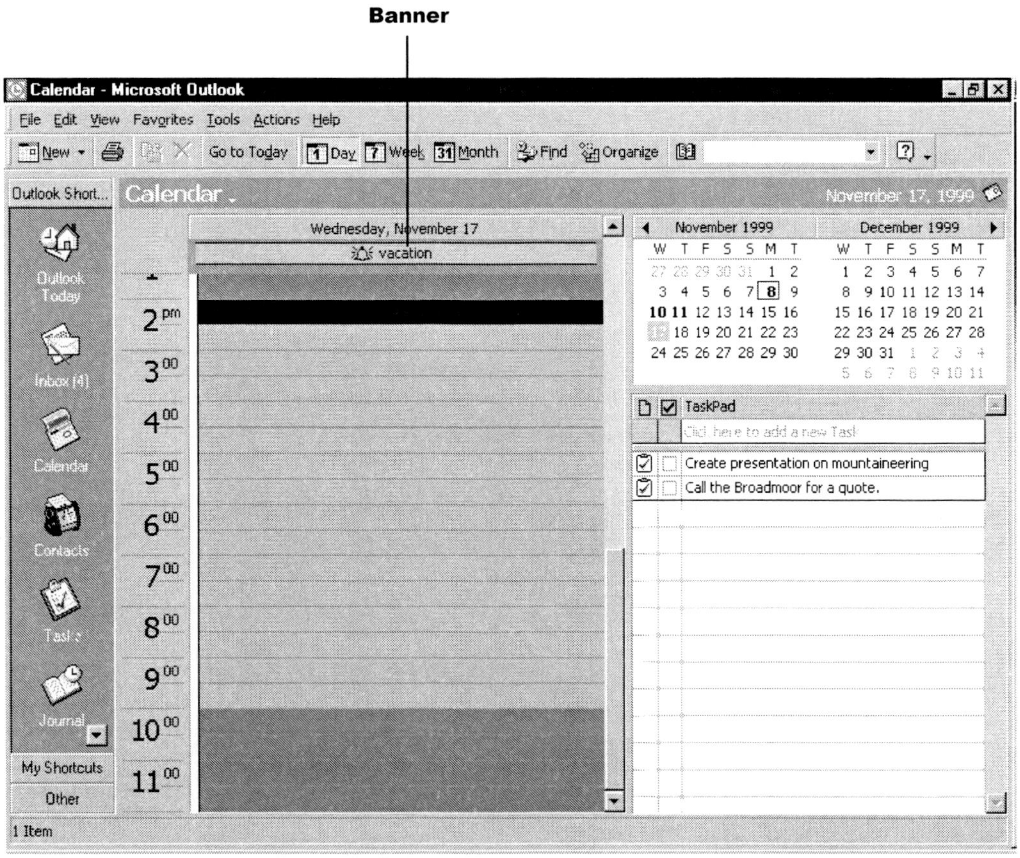

To schedule a multi-day event:

❶ In the Calendar, display the day that you want to schedule an event.

❷ Click the New Appointment button on the toolbar.

❸ Type a subject in the Subject text box.

❹ Specify a Start time and End time.

❺ If the event will last all day for each day that the event spans, select the All day event check box.

❻ Select options as desired.

❼ Click the Save and Close button.

TRY IT 4–4 — SCHEDULE A MULTI-DAY EVENT

In this exercise, you will schedule a week vacation as an event.

---

1. Display next Friday.

2. Schedule an event that spans three days.

CLICK: The **New Appointment** [New] button on the toolbar.

An Appointment window appears.

TYPE: **vacation**

CLICK: The **End Time** drop-down arrow and click the following Friday.

THEN: Select the all day event check box.

CLICK: The Show time as drop-down arrow, and click **Out of Office**.

The event options are specified.

CLICK: The **Save and Close** button.

The event is set. The banner titled "vacation" appears under the date.

TIP

You can delete an event by right-clicking it in the Calendar, and clicking **Delete** on the shortcut menu.

Notice that a purple bar is displayed to the left of the first day of the vacation. This is the same purple bar that someone on your network will see if he or she adds your name as an attendee to a meeting (if they use the Attendee Availability tab in the Meeting window to schedule a meeting). If you display the Meeting window, and click the Attendee Availability tab, you will see that the purple bar means that you are out of the office. (A light blue bar indicates that you could tentatively join a meeting at that time, and a dark blue bar means that you are busy, so you wouldn't be able to attend a meeting at that time.)

THEN: Display a few days after Friday (within the seven day vacation you just scheduled).

Each day appears with a purple bar to the left of it, and a vacation banner under the date.

Microsoft also provides a tool, called NetShow, that can be used to watch broadcasts over the Web. Companies use NetShow to broadcast product presentations, training presentations, and any other multimedia presentation that benefits from multimedia features but does not require interactivity (as does NetMeeting). You can schedule a NetShow broadcast just as you schedule a meeting in Calendar. Invite attendees just as you normally would for a NetMeeting.

Using the Calendar on the Web

For Your Information

You can save a Calendar as a Web page to share it with others. The events coordinator at Lakewood Mountain Resort saved a calendar displaying an employee volleyball schedule, so that anyone who wanted to view it, could simply type the calendar's Web address in a browser to access it.

Saving a Calendar as a Web Page

When you save the Calendar as a Web page, Outlook converts the Calendar to *HTML*. Simply put, HTML is the markup language that is used to display documents on the Internet.

Before you save your Calendar as a Web page, you must schedule the appointments that you want to display.

To save a calendar as a Web page:

1. Add appointments to the Calendar as necessary.
2. Click File on the menu bar.
3. Click Save as Web Page on the File menu to display the Save as Web Page dialog box as displayed on the following page.

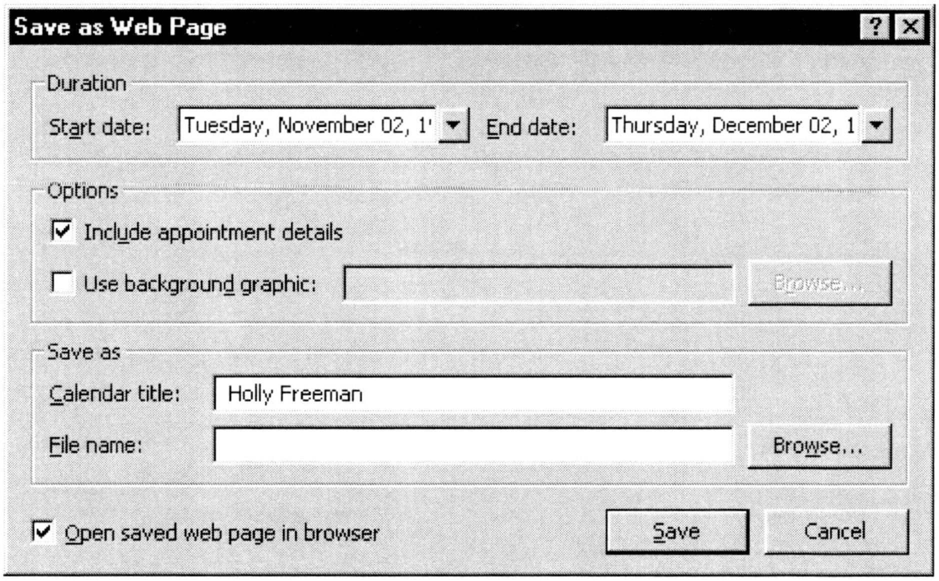

❹ In the Duration section, specify a Start date and End date.

❺ In the Options section, specify options.

❻ In the Calendar title text box select the current text and type a title for the Calendar.

❼ Click the Browse button to navigate to a location, and type a file name in the File name text box.

❽ Click Save.

TRY IT 4–5 — SAVE THE CALENDAR AS A WEB PAGE

In this exercise, you will create a recurring appointment for a volleyball game. You will then save a calendar as a Web page.

> You must install the Web publishing feature for the steps in this exercise to work correctly.

1. **Create a recurring appointment.**

   FIRST: Display the first Tuesday of next month.

   CLICK: The **New Appointment** [New] button on the toolbar.

An Appointment window is displayed.

TYPE: **Volleyball**

CLICK: In the Location text box, and type **West Gym**.

CLICK: The **Recurrence** button.

The Appointment Recurrence dialog box appears as shown below:

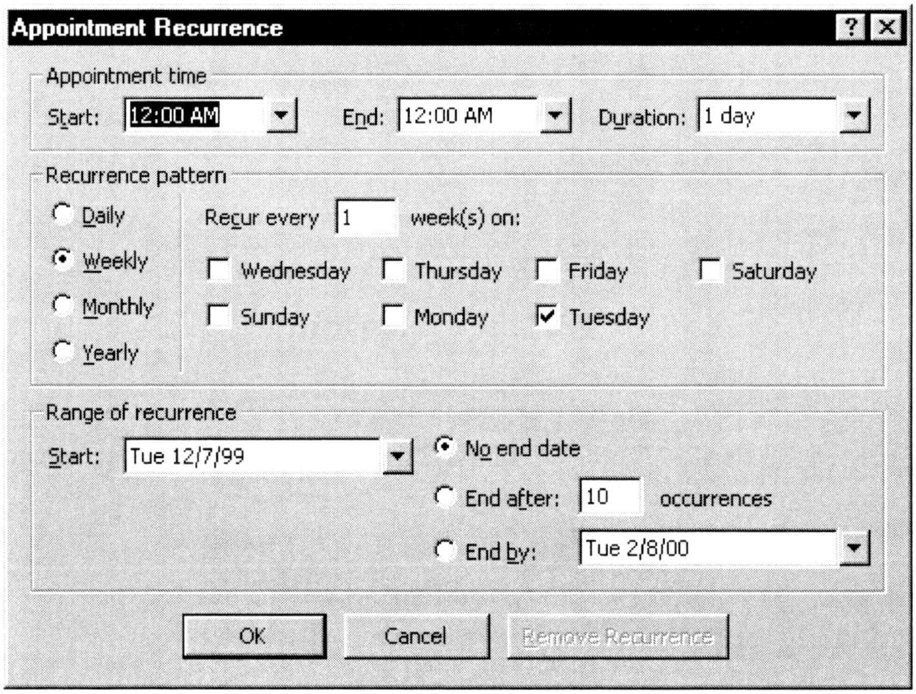

CLICK: The Start drop-down arrow in the Appointment time section, scroll down, if necessary, and click **7:30 P.M.**

CLICK: The End drop-down arrow, and click **8:30 P.M.**

Notice that the duration is automatically set to one hour.

THEN: In the Range of recurrence section, click the End by option.

NEXT: Select the text in the End by text box.

TYPE: **the last Tuesday in month**

CLICK: **OK**

The Recurring Appointment window appears, displaying the recurrence options you specified.

CLICK: The **Save and Close** button.

The Volleyball appointment appears in the Calendar.

2. Save the Calendar as a Web page.

CLICK: **File** on the menu bar.

CLICK: **Save as Web Page** on the File menu.

The Save as Web Page dialog box is displayed.

CLICK: The Start date drop-down arrow and click the first Tuesday in the next month.

CLICK: The End date drop-down arrow and click the last Tuesday in the next month.

THEN: In the Calendar title text box, select the current text and type **Employee Volleyball**.

CLICK: The **Browse** button, navigate to the Outlook Intermediate folder, and type **Employee Volleyball** in the File name text box.

CLICK: The **Select** button.

CLICK: The **Save** button.

The calendar is saved as a Web page and appears in Internet Explorer.

If Internet Explorer does not automatically display the Web calendar, you can manually open the calendar in the Exploring window. (Display the Exploring window. Navigate to the Outlook Intermediate folder. Double-click the Employee Volleyball folder. You will notice that there are many files that were created as a result of creating the Web calendar. Double-click the file called Employee Volleyball.htm. Internet Explorer will then open and display the Web calendar.)

SHARING THE CALENDAR OVER THE INTERNET

For Your Information

You can use iCalendar (Internet Calendaring) to send meeting requests to people over the Internet. iCalendar is a component of Outlook that allows you to share whether you are free or busy at certain times during the day with people over the Internet. With iCalendar, you can send meeting requests and receive responses from invitees.

> **To use the iCalender feature properly, you must send a meeting request to someone who uses an iCalendar compliant mail program.**

When you send a meeting request over the Internet, Outlook sends an iCalendar attachment that contains the meeting information. When an invitee receives a meeting request, he or she can open or download the attachment, and can accept or decline the invitation. If the invitee accepts, he or she can then add the meeting to his or her own calendar.

To share the Calendar with other applications over the Internet:

❶ Create a meeting.

❷ In the Meeting window, click Actions on the menu bar.

❸ Click Forward as iCalendar.

❹ Enter the address of the recipient in the To text box.

❺ Click the Send button.

❻ Click the Close button in the top-right corner of the window.

❼ Click Yes in the alert box that appears.

TRY IT 4–6 — SHARE THE CALENDAR USING ICALENDAR

In this exercise, you will create a meeting and send the meeting as an iCalendar attachment to your class partner.

---

1. **Display the Monday after next in Day view.**

2. **Create a meeting.**

   CLICK: The 12 P.M. line in the Calendar.

   CLICK: The drop-down arrow to the right of the New Appointment button on the toolbar.

   CLICK: **Meeting Request**

   The Meeting window is displayed.

   CLICK: The **To** button.

   The Select Attendees and Resources dialog box appears.

   THEN: If necessary, scroll and click your class partner's name.

   CLICK: The **Required** button.

   CLICK: **OK**

   The meeting request is going to be sent to your class partner.

   CLICK: In the Subject text box, and type **Ski Club Meeting**.

   CLICK: In the Location text box, and type **Lakewood Mountain Resort Lounge**.

   CLICK: The second End time drop-down arrow, and click **1:00 P.M. (1 hour)**.

3. **Send the meeting as an iCalendar attachment.**

   FIRST: In the Meeting window, click **Actions** on the menu bar.

   CLICK: **Forward as iCalendar**

   A message window appears. Your class partner's e-mail address is already inserted.

CLICK: The **Send** button.

The meeting request will be sent to your class partner.

CLICK: The **Close** button in the top-right corner of the message window.

An alert box appears, asking if you want to save changes.

CLICK: **No**

Normally you would click Yes in the alert box so that the meeting would appear in your Calendar, but because your class partner is going to send this same meeting request to you, you need your calendar to be open on this day for this exercise to work properly. Otherwise, when you open the iCalendar attachment from your partner, a meeting window will appear, alerting you that you already have a meeting on that day (the meeting you tried to schedule). This is not the result that you would normally see. By clicking No, you will be able to be both the meeting organizer and the invitee. Obviously, in the real world, you would never be both at the same time. This is only used for classroom purposes.

4. Open the iCalendar your class partner sent to you.

FIRST: Display the Inbox.

CLICK: The **Send/Receive** button on the toolbar.

THEN: Open the attachment in the Ski Club Meeting message.

A window similar to the one on the next page appears.

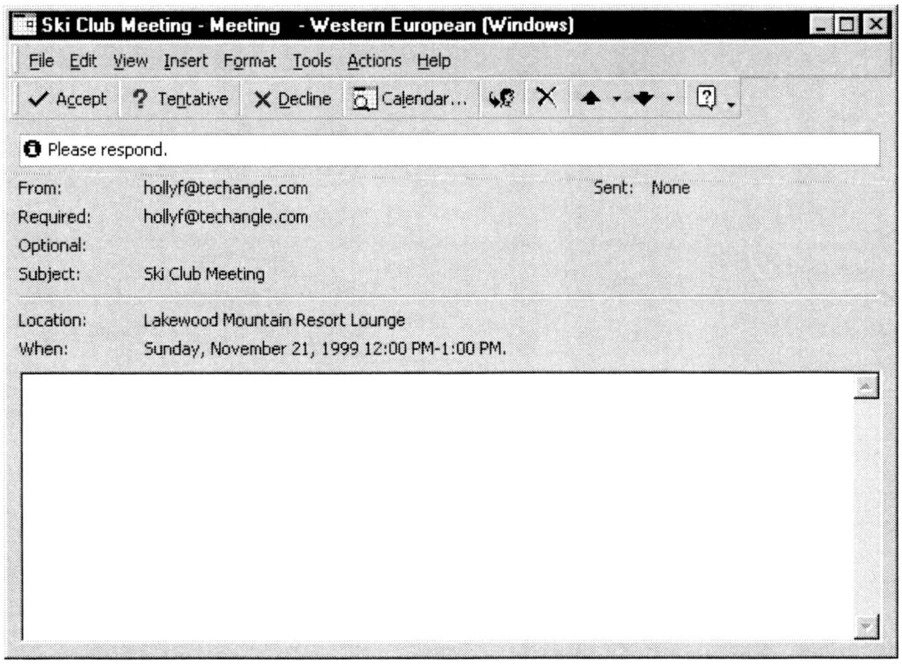

5. **Accept the invitation to the meeting.**

CLICK: The **Accept** [Accept] button on the toolbar.

An alert box appears, informing you that the meeting will be added to your Calendar, and asking if you want to include comments with your response. The Send response now option is already selected.

CLICK: **OK**

CLICK: The **Send/Receive** [Send/Receive] button.

An e-mail message appears in your Inbox stating that your class partner accepted.

THEN: Display the Calendar.

NEXT: Display the Monday after next in the Calendar.

The meeting is added to your Calendar.

After the response is sent, the meeting organizer can see who has responded to the meeting by double-clicking the meeting in the Calendar, clicking the Attendee Availability tab, and clicking the Show attendee status option.

QuickLook at Lesson 4

To	Do This
Configure Calendar options	**1.** Click **Tools** on the menu bar. **2.** Click **Options** on the Tools menu. **3.** Click the **Calendar Options** button to display the Calendar Options dialog box. **4.** Change options as desired. **5.** Click **OK** twice.
Schedule a meeting	**1.** In the Calendar, display the day that you want to schedule a meeting. **2.** Click the drop-down arrow to the right of the New Appointment button on the toolbar. **3.** Click **Meeting Request** to display the Meeting window. **4.** Click the **To** button. **5.** Choose prospective attendees by clicking a contact or clicking a group, and then clicking either the **Required** or **Optional** buttons, and clicking **OK**. **6.** Click in the Subject text box and type a subject. **7.** Click in the Location text box and type the location where the meeting will be held. **8.** Modify the Start time and End time options as desired. **9.** Click the **Send** button.
Schedule real-time meetings	**1.** In the Calendar, display the day that you want to schedule a NetMeeting. **2.** Click the drop-down arrow to the right of the New Appointment button on the toolbar. **3.** Click **Meeting Request**. **4.** Click the **To** button. **5.** Choose prospective attendees by clicking a contact or clicking a group, and then clicking either the **Required** or **Optional** buttons, and clicking **OK**. **6.** Click in the Subject text box and type a subject. **7.** Select the This is an online meeting using check box. **8.** If necessary click the This is an online meeting using drop-down arrow, and click **Windows NetMeeting**. **9.** Modify options as desired. **10.** Click the **Send** button.

To	Do This
Schedule a multi-day event	**1.** In the Calendar, display the day that you want to schedule an event. **2.** Click the **New Appointment** button on the toolbar. **3.** Type a subject in the Subject text box. **4.** Specify a Start time and End time. **5.** If the event will last all day for each day that the event spans, select the All day event check box. **6.** Select options as desired. **7.** Click the **Save and Close** button.
Save a calendar as a Web page	**1.** Add appointments to the Calendar as necessary. **2.** Click **File** on the menu bar. **3.** Click **Save as Web Page** on the File menu to display the Save as Web Page dialog box. **4.** In the Duration section, specify a Start date and End date. **5.** In the Options section, specify options. **6.** In the Calendar title text box select the current text, and type a title for the Calendar. **7.** Click the **Browse** button to navigate to a location, and type a file name in the File name text box. **8.** Click **Save**.
Share the Calendar with other applications over the Internet	**1.** Create a meeting. **2.** In the Meeting window, click **Actions** on the menu bar. **3.** Click **Forward as iCalendar**. **4.** Enter the address of the recipient in the To text box. **5.** Click the **Send** button. **6.** Click the **Close** button in the top-right corner of the window. **7.** Click **Yes** in the alert box that appears.

SkillCheck – Lesson 4

1. Change the Calendar options so that the work week starts on a Monday and ends on a Friday, 8:00 A.M. to 5:00 P.M., and the week numbers are displayed in the Date Navigator.

2. Invite your class partner to a meeting about Outlook 2000, which will be held in the auditorium the first Monday of next month from 9:00 A.M. to 10:00 A.M.

3. Invite your class partner to a real-time meeting about Windows NetMeeting, which will be held the second Tuesday of next month from 1:00 P.M. to 2:00 P.M.

4. Schedule an all-day four-day seminar about wilderness survival, starting next Friday.

5. Create a basket weaving class schedule two months into the future for every Thursday during that month from 9:00 P.M. to 10:00 P.M.

6. Publish the basket weaving class schedule on the Web.

7. Invite someone in your class (other than your class partner) to a meeting about a Canned Food Drive, which will be held in the parking lot the first Thursday next month from noon to 12:15 P.M., using iCalendar.

Answers to the SkillChecks can be found here: **http://www.activeed.com/skanswers/outlook2.htm**

Performance Objectives

You will learn how to:

- Manage contacts
- Sort contacts
- Use contacts to create mailing labels and perform a mail merge in Microsoft Word
- Create a form for contacts

For Your Information

You can manage contacts in a couple ways. You can a *flag* a contact so that you can remind yourself to perform an action, such as call or e-mail the contact. You can also sort your contacts within various views by different fields so that you can facilitate finding contacts.

Flagging Contacts for Follow Up

To flag a contact, you can specify what your action is by clicking an option in the list provided for you, or you can type your own action, such as "Send flowers" or "Buy wedding gift." You can also specify by what time the action needs to take place, so that Outlook will send you a reminder to perform the action.

After you flag a contact, the contact will be displayed with the text "Flag for Follow Up: [description of the action that you are supposed to perform]". When you have performed the action, simply right-click the contact and click Flag Complete.

If you forget to perform the action, or if you simply forget to mark the flag as complete, after the due date has passed, the contact information will appear in red until you mark the flag as complete.

To flag contacts for follow up:

❶ Select or open a contact.

❷ Click the Flag For Follow Up button on the toolbar to display the Flag for Follow Up dialog box, as shown on the next page.

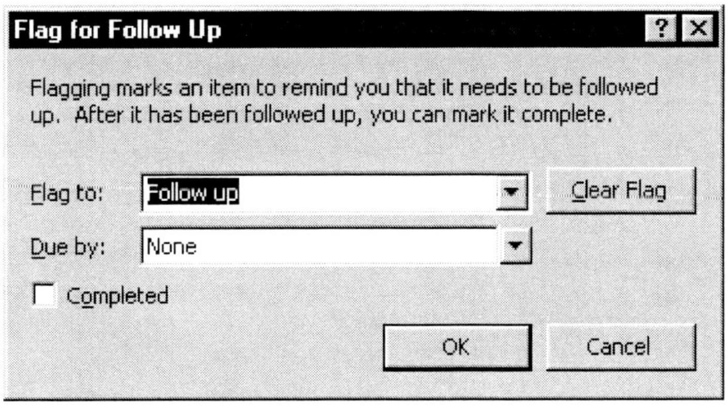

❸ Click the Flag to drop-down arrow, and click an option.

Or

Type an action.

❹ Click the Due by drop-down arrow, and click a date.

❺ Click OK.

To mark a flag as complete:

❶ Right-click the flagged contact.

❷ Click Flag Complete on the shortcut menu.

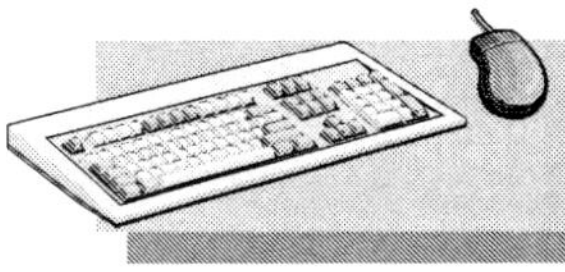

TRY IT 5–1 — FLAG CONTACTS FOR FOLLOW UP

In this exercise, you will flag the contact Kate Cadrow to remind yourself to call her by tomorrow; you will flag the contact Amy Isaacson to remind yourself to send her flowers by Monday of next week; and then you will flag the contact John Chesbro to remind yourself to send a birthday card to him by Tuesday of next week. You will then mark the flag for Kate Cadrow as completed.

---

1. **Display the Contacts folder.**
2. **Flag contacts.**

   CLICK: The contact Kate Cadrow.

CLICK: The **Flag for Follow Up** button on the toolbar.

The Flag for Follow Up dialog box is displayed.

CLICK: The Flag to drop-down arrow, and click **Call**.

CLICK: The Due by drop-down arrow, and click tomorrow's date.

CLICK: **OK**

The text *Follow Up Flag: Call* appears under the contact's name.

DOUBLE-CLICK: The contact Kate Cadrow.

A message appears in the Contact window, stating that you need to call Kate by tomorrow.

THEN: Close the Contact window.

CLICK: The contact Amy Isaacson.

CLICK: The **Flag for Follow Up** button on the toolbar.

The Flag for Follow Up dialog box is displayed.

TYPE: **Send flowers**

CLICK: The Due by drop-down arrow, and click Monday of next week.

CLICK: **OK**

The text *Follow Up Flag: Send flowers* appears under the contacts name.

DOUBLE-CLICK: The contact Amy Isaacson.

A message appears in the Contact window, stating that you need to send flowers to Amy by next Monday.

THEN: Close the Contact window.

CLICK: The contact John Chesbro.

CLICK: The **Flag for Follow Up** button on the toolbar.

The Flag for Follow Up dialog box is displayed.

TIP

You can use the contacts window to link the current contact to an activity. After you link the contacts, you can click the **Activities** tab and see that the contact is linked to the activity you specified. To link contacts to activities, in the Contact window, click **Actions**, point to **Link**, and click **Items**. In the Look in list, click a folder that contains activities, and in the Items list, click an item, and click **OK**.

TYPE: **Send birthday card**

CLICK: The Due by drop-down arrow, and click Tuesday of next week.

CLICK: **OK**

The text *Follow Up Flag: Send birthday card* appears under the contacts name.

DOUBLE-
CLICK: The contact John Chesbro.

A message appears in the Contact window, stating that you need to send a birthday card to John by next Tuesday.

THEN: Close the Contact window.

3. **Mark a flag as completed.**

TIP

You can clear a flag so that there is no longer a record of it by right-clicking the contact, and clicking **Clear Flag**.

RIGHT-
CLICK: The contact Kate Cadrow.

CLICK: **Flag Complete**

DOUBLE-
CLICK: The contact Kate Cadrow.

A message appears in the Contact window, describing the action that you had to perform, and when the action was completed.

THEN: Close the Contact window.

Sorting Contacts

In Lesson 1, you sorted contacts in the By Category view. You clicked a column heading such as Full Name or Company to display the items related to that heading in ascending or descending order. You can use the same method for sorting contacts in the following views: Phone List, By Company, By Location, and By Follow-up Flag.

Because the Address Cards view (the default) and Detailed Address Cards view are not in a table format, which has column headings at the top of the contacts list, you sort the contacts in these views a little differently. You use the Sort dialog box to sort contacts in the Address Cards and Detailed Address Cards views.

The Sort dialog box allows you to sort contacts by more than one criterion. For example, the marketing director at Lakewood Mountain Resort wanted to find a contact that he knew didn't have an e-mail address, and knew that the contact's last name started with the letter "R." To facilitate finding this contact, he sorted the contacts by e-mail address in ascending order, which displayed all of the contacts without an e-mail address at the top of the contact list; however in no particular order. He further sorted the contacts by last name in descending order, which caused the contacts without e-mail addresses to appear in alphabetical order. This brought the marketing director's target contact even closer to the top of the contact list, thus making the contact even more accessible.

To sort contacts:

● Click the column heading that you want to sort by to toggle between ascending and descending order.

Or

❶ Right-click a blank area of the contact list, and click Sort to display the Sort dialog box as shown below:

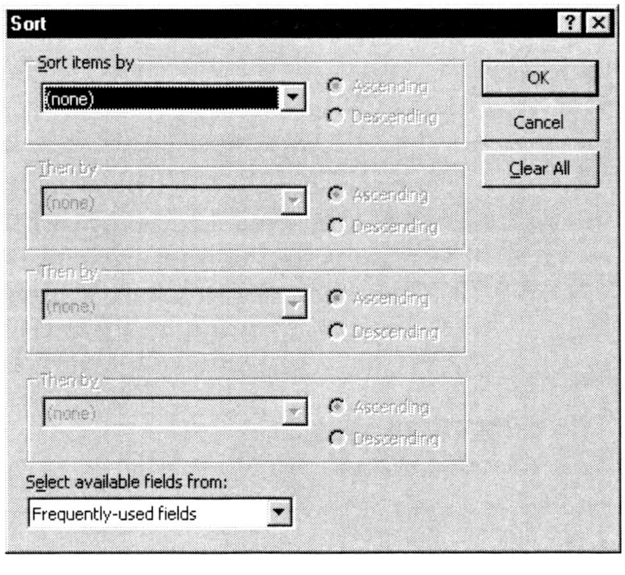

❷ Click the Sort items by drop-down arrow, click an item, and click the Ascending or Descending option.

❸ If desired, click the Then by drop-down arrow, click an item, and click the Ascending or Descending option.

❹ If desired, to change the field sets displayed in the Sort items by and Then by lists, click the Select available fields from drop-down arrow, and click a new field set.

❺ Click OK.

> You can customize the appearance of the menus and toolbars in the Contacts folder by right-clicking a toolbar or menu name and clicking Customize (the Customize dialog box will appear). On the Toolbars tab, you can add or remove toolbars. On the Commands tab, you can click a category in the Categories list, and drag a command onto a toolbar or menu. Conversely, you can drag a command off of the toolbar or menu when the Customize dialog box is displayed. Finally, on the Options tab, you can click the Reset my usage data button to restore the toolbar and menus to their default settings. You can also display the toolbar buttons with large icons, turn off the options to list font names in their font, show ScreenTips on toolbars, show shortcut keys in ScreenTips, and turn on various menu animations.

Try It 5–2 — Sort Contacts

In this exercise, you will sort contacts in the By Follow-up Flag view. You will then sort the contacts in the Address Cards view.

---

1. Display the Contacts folder in By Follow-up Flag view.

CLICK: **View** on the menu bar.

THEN: Point to **Current View**.

CLICK: **By Follow-up Flag**

> The contacts are now in By Follow-up Flag view. Notice that the flag that has been completed is now grayed out, and the flags that have not been marked as completed are red.

2. **Sort the contacts by flag status.**

CLICK: The **Sort by: Flag Status** column heading.

The flags are moved to the end of the list of contacts and are sorted by flag status.

CLICK: The **Sort by: Flag Status** column heading again.

The flags are moved to the top of the list and are sorted by flag status.

3. **Sort the contacts by company.**

CLICK: The **Sort by: Company** column heading.

The flagged items remain at the top of the list and the contacts are sorted in ascending order by company.

4. **Sort the contacts by last name.**

CLICK: The **Sort by: File As** column heading.

The flagged items remain at the top of the list and the contacts are sorted in ascending order by last name.

5. **Display the contacts in Address Cards view.**

CLICK: **View** on the menu bar.

THEN: Point to **Current View**.

CLICK: **Address Cards**

The contacts are displayed in address cards.

6. **Sort the address cards.**

RIGHT-CLICK: A blank area of the contacts list.

CLICK: **Sort**

The Sort dialog box appears.

CLICK: The Sort items by drop-down arrow.

THEN: Scroll up and click **E-mail**.

NEXT: In the Sort items by section, click the Descending option.

CLICK: **OK**

The contacts are sorted in descending order by e-mail address.

THEN: Scroll to the end of the contacts list by dragging the horizontal scroll bar to the right.

Notice that contacts that do not have e-mail addresses are at the end of the list. These contacts are not displayed in any particular order.

7. Add another sort criterion to the current sort.

RIGHT-CLICK: A blank area of the contact list.

CLICK: **Sort**

The Sort dialog box appears. Your current settings are still applied.

TIP

You can clear the current options by clicking the **Clear All** button in the Sort dialog box.

CLICK: The Then by drop-down arrow.

THEN: Scroll down and click **File As**.

CLICK: **OK**

The contacts that do not have e-mail messages are sorted by last name in ascending order.

Use Contacts to Create Mailing Labels

For Your Information

You can use your contacts to create various files such as form letters, mailing labels, or envelopes. You achieve this by merging contact information into Microsoft Word documents.

Understanding Mail Merge

The mail merge process primarily deals with three elements: the *main document,* the *data source*, and the *fields* within the data source. The main document is a file that contains fixed text, such as the body of a form letter, or the formatting used to create a document, such as mailing labels. The data source contains text that has information that varies, such as the information for each contact in your Contacts folder. The fields are the categories in the data source, such as first name, last name, home address, home phone, and so on that will be inserted in the main document during the merge process. When you perform a merge, you integrate these elements to create a single file containing an item for each contact, such as a letter or a label.

For example, the marketing director at Lakewood Mountain Resort created a form letter about giving a birthday discount to guests. The first thing he did was create the letter in Microsoft Word. He wrote the form letter, like any other letter, except he left out any text that would change, such as a name of a contact that would come after the word "Dear," and the date that would come after the text "Because your birthday was on…." After he completed the letter, he used Outlook to display only the guests that he wanted to send this letter to. During the mail merge process, he then inserted the relevant contact fields into the form letter, such as the First Name field after the word Dear, and the Birthday field after the text "Because your birthday was on …." After he completed the merge, a personalized letter for each contact was created.

Using Contacts to Create Mailing Labels in Word

You don't need to create a main document for some mail merges you perform. For example, Outlook lets you generate mailing labels without having to create a mailing label main document. The mailing label document is created by Word as you perform the mail merge.

Preparing for a Mail Merge

You can do a few things to prepare your contacts and fields for the Mail Merge Contacts dialog box: You can display or select certain contacts that you want to merge. You can also choose to display only certain fields that are relevant to the merge document that you are going to create.

Before you merge contacts into a Word document, you should select or display only those contacts that you want to merge, because most likely, you probably won't want to merge every contact. For example, each month, the marketing assistant at Lakewood Mountain Resort sends thank you cards to guests from a specific state. This month, she decided to send cards to guests from California, so she filtered out all other contacts so that they would not be included in the merge. You could use the Filter dialog box to filter contacts. You could also filter contacts by simply selecting each contact that you wanted to include in the merge by pressing Alt and then clicking each contact to be included. Finally, you could filter contacts by creating a custom folder that would contain only certain contacts, and display that folder before you perform the merge.

When you create mailing labels, the only information that you need in order to successfully create them is the names and addresses of the contacts. Outlook has over a hundred fields for you to choose from, such as Manager's name, Birthday, and Anniversary. Obviously, these are not fields you would put on mailing labels. In the Mail Merge Contacts dialog box, you will have the option to make all these fields available to you during the merge, or to make only specified fields available. To avoid having to scroll through over a hundred unnecessary fields, you can add or remove fields from whatever Outlook view you happen to be in, then click the Contact fields in current view option in the Mail Merge Contacts dialog box.

To add or remove fields in the current view:

1. Right-click a blank area of the Contacts list.
2. Click Show Fields.
3. In the Show these fields in this order list, click a field and click the Remove button.

   Or

   In the Available fields list click a field and click the Add button.
4. Repeat step 3 as necessary.
5. Click OK.

Performing a Mail Merge

You use the Mail Merge Contacts dialog box to start the mail merge process. You should have a good understanding about what each option will do if you select it. The following table details the options that you can choose in the Mail Merge Contacts dialog box:

Option	What it does
All contacts in current view	All the contacts in your current view will be included in the mail merge. If you filter your contacts, or put contacts in a custom folder only the visible contacts will be merged.
Only selected contacts	Only the contact(s) that you select will be included in the mail merge. You can select multiple non-consecutive contacts by pressing Ctrl, then clicking the desired contacts. If you select any contacts, this option will already be selected for you.
All contact fields	Outlook will export over a hundred fields for you to choose from during the merge process.

Option	What It Does
Contact fields in current view	Outlook will export only the fields that are displayed in the current view. If you are going to create labels, then you would probably want to choose this option so that you don't have to sort through over a hundred fields during the merge process.
New document	Microsoft Word will create a new document as a result of the merge. An existing document is not necessary.
Existing document	You will use an existing document, such as a form letter that you created in Microsoft Word, to merge the contact information into.
Permanent file	A contact data file is created, which will store your contact information used for the current mail merge for use for a future mail merge.
Document type	Lets you create the following document types: form letters, mailing labels, envelopes, or catalogs.
Merge to	Specifies the type of mail merge. You can create a new document file, you can send the merge directly to the printer, you can create an e-mail form letter, or a fax.

To use contacts to create mailing labels:

❶ Open the Contacts folder that you want to use. If desired, filter your contacts and/or select contacts.

❷ Click Tools on the menu bar.

❸ Click Mail Merge on the Tools menu to display the Mail Merge Contacts dialog box as shown below:

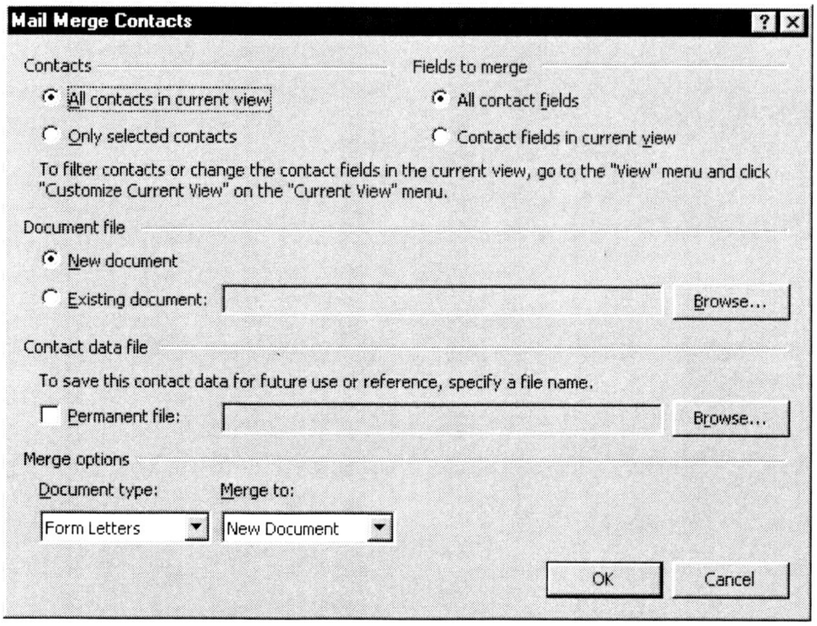

❹ In the Contacts section, click the desired option.

❺ In the Fields to merge section, click the desired option.

❻ In the Document file section, click the desired option.

❼ In the Contact data file section, click the desired option.

❽ In the Merge options section, click the Document type drop-down arrow, and click Mailing Labels. Then click the merge to drop-down arrow, and click an option.

❾ Click OK.

Microsoft Word opens and the Office Assistant appears.

❿ Click the Complete Setup option.

⓫ If an alert box appears, click OK.

⓬ Click the Setup button to display the Label Options dialog box, as shown on the next page.

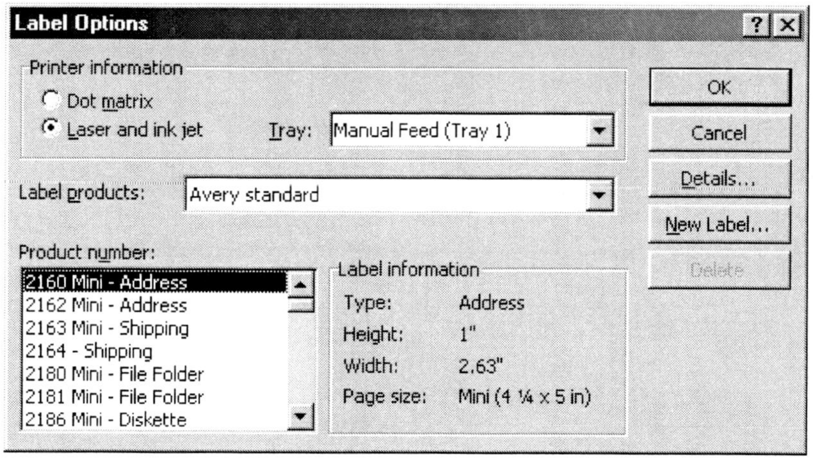

⓭ Select options as desired.

⓮ Click OK to display the Create Labels dialog box as shown below:

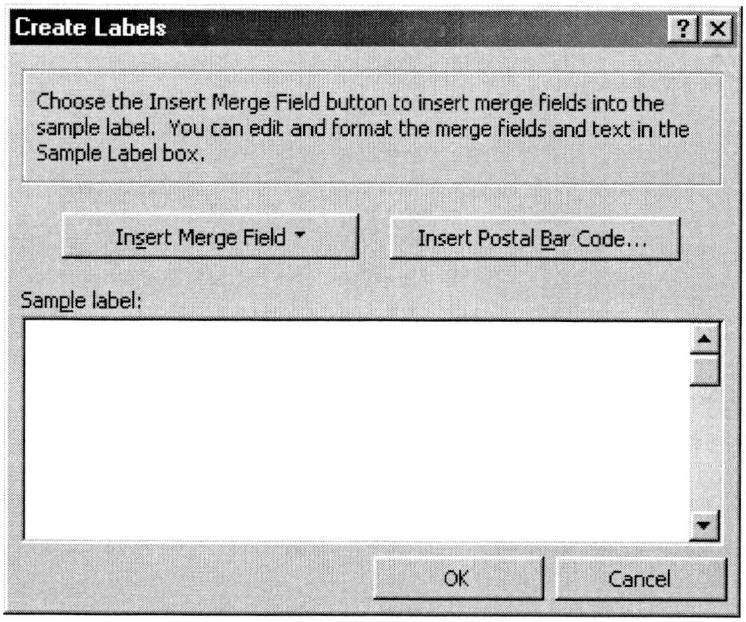

⓯ Click the Insert Merge Field button, and select the first field name for the label.

⓰ Repeat the previous step until all the fields are entered. (Make sure you add any necessary spaces and punctuation).

⓱ Click OK.

⓲ Click the Merge button.

⑲ In the Merge dialog box, click the Merge button.

⑳ Print and/or save the completed labels.

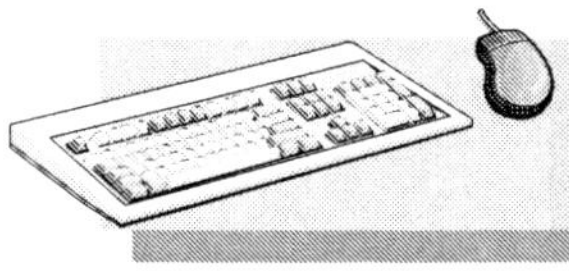

TRY IT 5-3 — USE MAIL MERGE

In this exercise, you will filter your contacts so that only contacts from California are displayed. Then you will use these contacts to create mailing labels.

---

1. Filter your contacts.

RIGHT-CLICK: A blank area of the Contacts list.

CLICK: **Filter**

The Filter dialog box appears.

TYPE: **CA**

CLICK: The In drop-down arrow, and click **address fields only**.

CLICK: The **More Choices** tab.

THEN: Select the Match case check box.

CLICK: **OK**

Contacts from California are displayed.

2. Display only the relevant fields.

RIGHT-CLICK: A blank area of the Contacts list.

CLICK: **Show Fields**

The Show Fields dialog box appears, as shown on the next page.

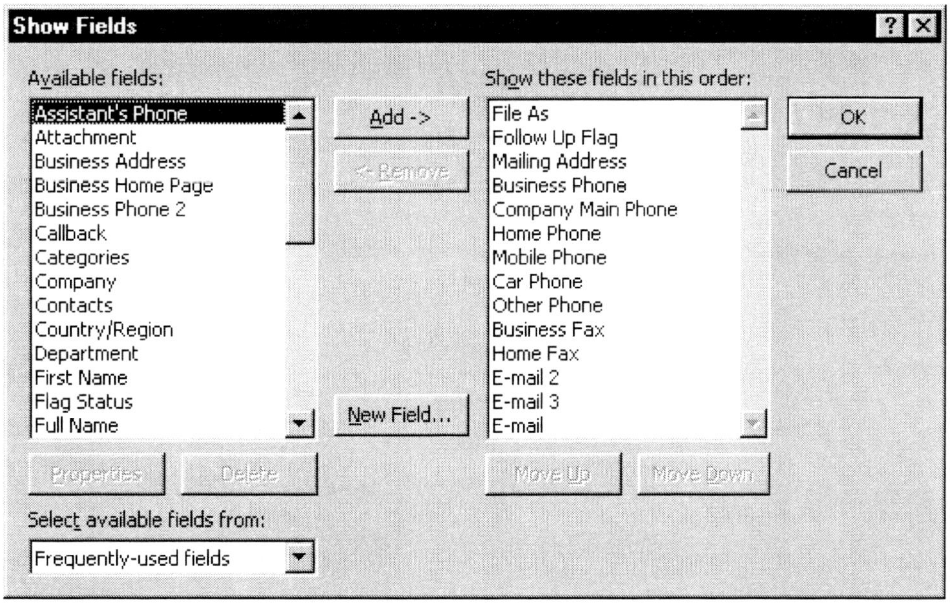

THEN: In the Show these fields in this order list, click **Follow Up Flag** and click the **Remove** button.

The field moves to the Available fields list.

THEN: In the Show these fields in this order list, click **E-mail** and click the **Remove** button.

The field moves to the Available fields list.

TIP

If you desire, you can add a bar code to the label. Click the **Insert Postal Bar Code** button, Click the Merge field with Zip code drop-down arrow, click **Zip_Code**, click the Merge field with street address drop-down arrow, click **Address_Line_1**, and click **OK**.

CLICK: **OK**

THEN: Using the same method, remove all fields except Mailing Address.

NEXT: In the Available fields list, click **Full Name**.

CLICK: The **Add** button.

CLICK: **OK**

Only the fields needed to for the mailing labels are displayed.

3. **Perform the merge.**

CLICK: **Tools** on the menu bar.

CLICK: **Mail Merge** on the Tools menu.

The Mail Merge Contacts dialog box appears. Notice that All contacts in current view is already selected.

THEN: In the Fields to merge section, click **Contact fields in current view**.

Notice that New document is already selected.

THEN: In the Merge option section, click the Document type drop-down arrow and click **Mailing Labels**.

CLICK: **OK**

Microsoft Word opens and the Office Assistant appears.

CLICK: The **Complete Setup** option.

The Mail Merge dialog box appears.

CLICK: The **Setup** button.

The Label Options dialog box appears.

4. **Specify a type of label to use.**

FIRST: Scroll down the Product number list, and click **8460 – Address**.

CLICK: **OK**

The Create Labels dialog box is displayed.

CLICK: The **Insert Merge Field** button.

A list of fields appears.

CLICK: **Full_Name** in the list.

The Full_Name field is inserted into the Sample label.

PRESS: **Enter**

CLICK: The **Insert Merge Field** button.

CLICK: **Mailing_Address** in the list.

The Mailing_Address merge field is inserted into the document.

CLICK: **OK**

5. **Perform the merge.**

CLICK: The **Merge** button.

The Merge dialog box is displayed.

CLICK: The **Merge** button.

The dialog box disappears, and the labels appear in a new document that looks similar to the figure below:

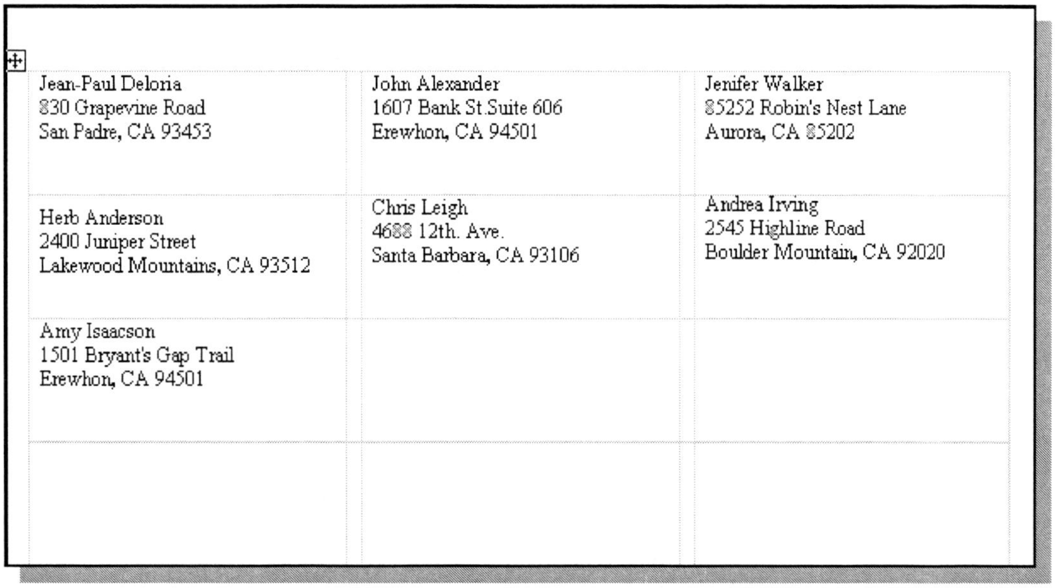

Jean-Paul Deloria 830 Grapevine Road San Padre, CA 93453	John Alexander 1607 Bank St.Suite 606 Erewhon, CA 94501	Jenifer Walker 85252 Robin's Nest Lane Aurora, CA 85202
Herb Anderson 2400 Juniper Street Lakewood Mountains, CA 93512	Chris Leigh 4688 12th. Ave. Santa Barbara, CA 93106	Andrea Irving 2545 Highline Road Boulder Mountain, CA 92020
Amy Isaacson 1501 Bryant's Gap Trail Erewhon, CA 94501		

6. **Print the labels.**

You would generally put labels in the printer using the product number of the labels you specified in the Label Options dialog box, but for classroom purposes you will print the labels on a regular sheet of paper.

CLICK: The **Print** button on the Standard toolbar.

7. **Close all open documents without saving.**

CREATING A FORM FOR CONTACTS

For Your Information

Every Outlook item is based on a form. For example, the window that you use to write e-mail messages is a form, as is the window that you use to schedule meetings. The window that appears when you open a contact is also a form. You can create a custom form that is based upon one of these forms.

Creating a Custom Form for Contacts

You can alter an existing Outlook form in various ways: You can delete unwanted fields, add new fields, rename existing fields, and move and resize fields. After you are finished altering a form you *publish* the form—meaning, you add the new form to Outlook. You can then use the form the same way you use any other Outlook form.

The customer service manager created a custom form for guests who stayed at Lakewood Mountain Resort. He used the existing form from the Contacts folder to add new fields, and remove unwanted fields. For example, he added a field called "Customer Complaints," so that he could record any complaints a guest might have had in order to improve Lakewood Mountain Resort, and to avoid future complaints concerning that same issue.

To create a custom form for contacts:

1. Open a new contact window.
2. Click Tools on the menu bar.
3. Point to Forms.
4. Click Design This Form to open the design window.
5. If desired, click a tab on the form that you want to change.
6. Make changes to the layout of the form by moving, resizing, adding, or deleting field labels and elements.

❼ When you are finished customizing the form, click the Publish Form button on the toolbar to display the Publish Form As dialog box as shown below:

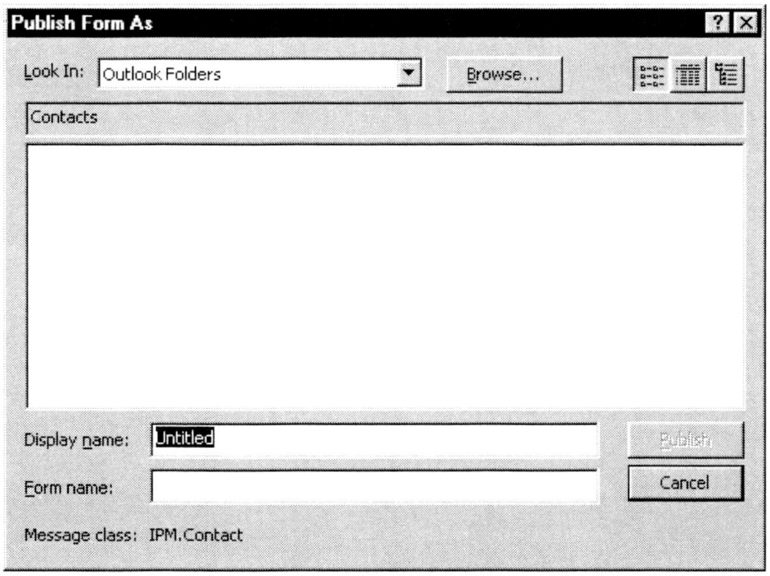

❽ Click the Look In drop-down arrow, and click Contacts.

❾ Click in the Display name text box, and type a display name.

❿ Click the Publish button.

To access a custom form:

❶ Click Actions on the menu bar.

❷ Click New [name of form] on the Actions menu.

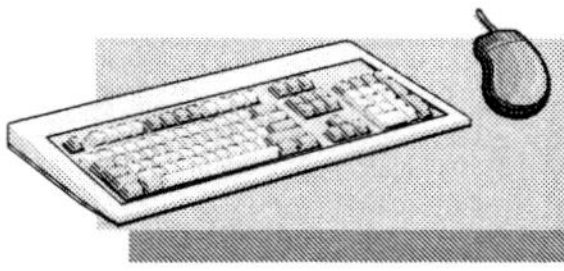

TRY IT 5–4 — CREATE A FORM FOR CONTACTS

In this exercise, you will create a custom form for Lakewood Mountain Resort Guests. You will then use the form.

---

1. Create a custom form.

FIRST: Open a new contact window.

CLICK: **Tools** on the menu bar.

THEN: Point to **Forms.**

CLICK: **Design This Form**

The design form window appears as shown below:

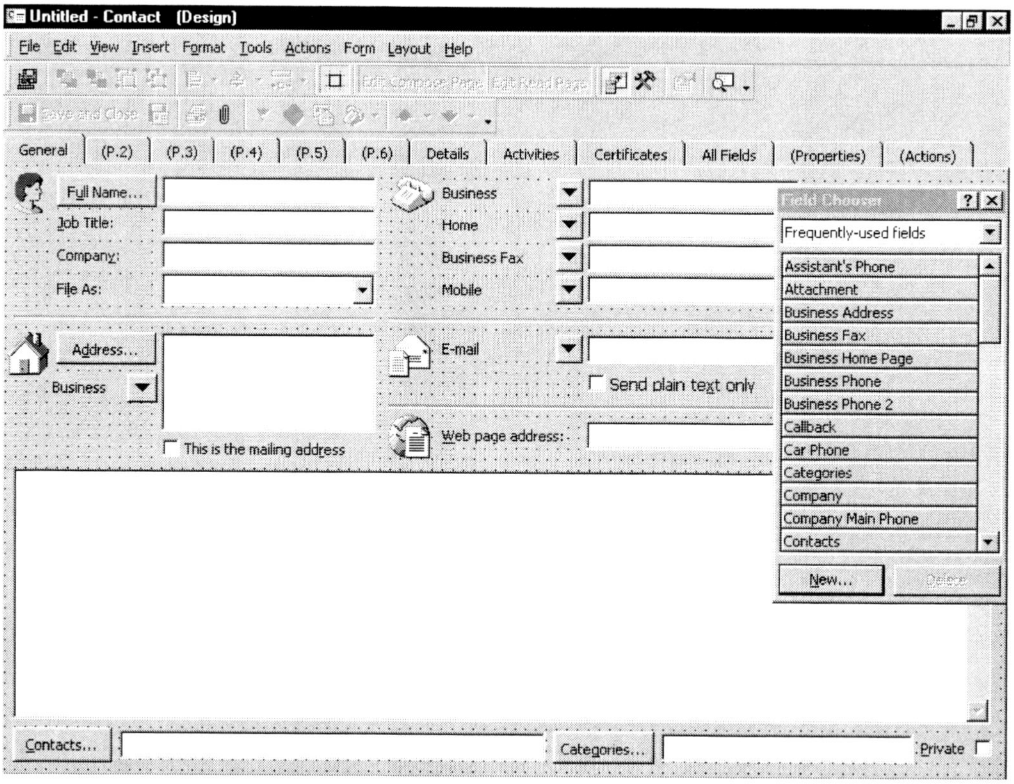

2. **Remove unwanted fields.**

CLICK: The Job Title text.

PRESS & HOLD: **Ctrl**

CLICK: The Job Title text box.

The text and the text box are selected.

PRESS: **Delete**

The text and the text box are deleted.

THEN: Using the same method as above, delete the following fields, text, text boxes, drop-down arrows, icons or buttons:

File As
Business
Business
This is the mailing address
Business Fax
Mobile
Web page address
Contacts
Categories

TIP

If you make a mistake, you can click **Edit** on the menu bar, and click **Undo** on the Edit menu.

Your form should now look similar to the following:

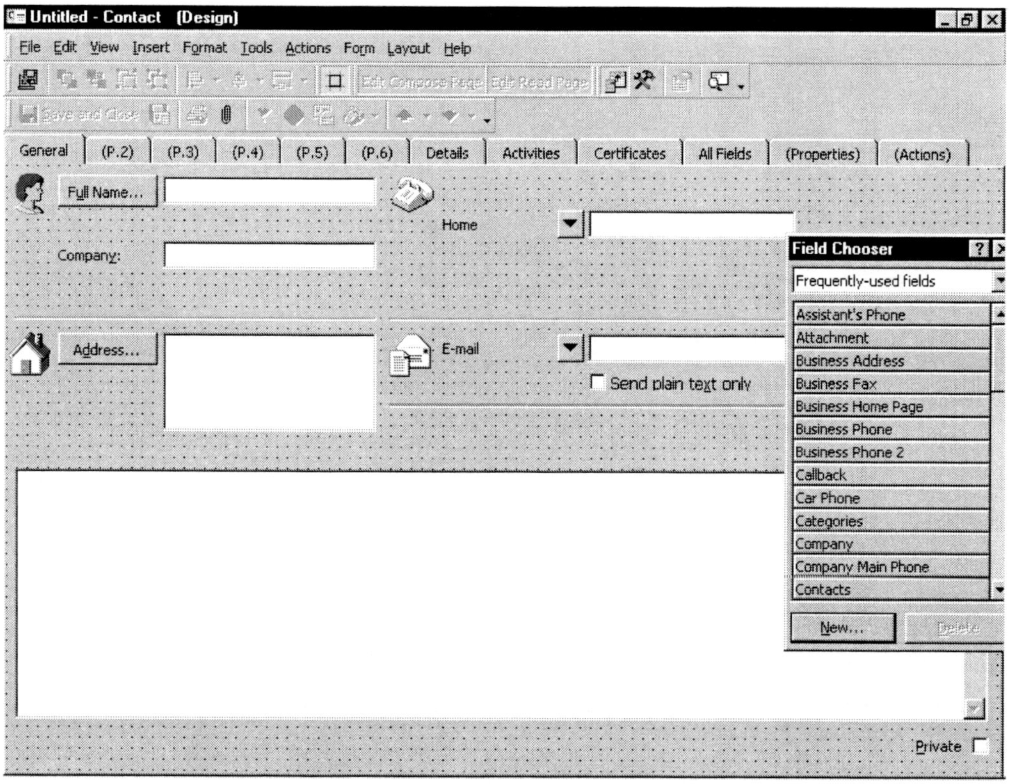

3. **Move fields.**

CLICK: The Company field.

THEN: Position the mouse pointer over one of the dotted borders around the text until the mouse pointer turns into a four-headed arrow ✥ (called a *move pointer*).

DRAG: The Company field down and to the left so that it appears just above the large white text box as shown below:

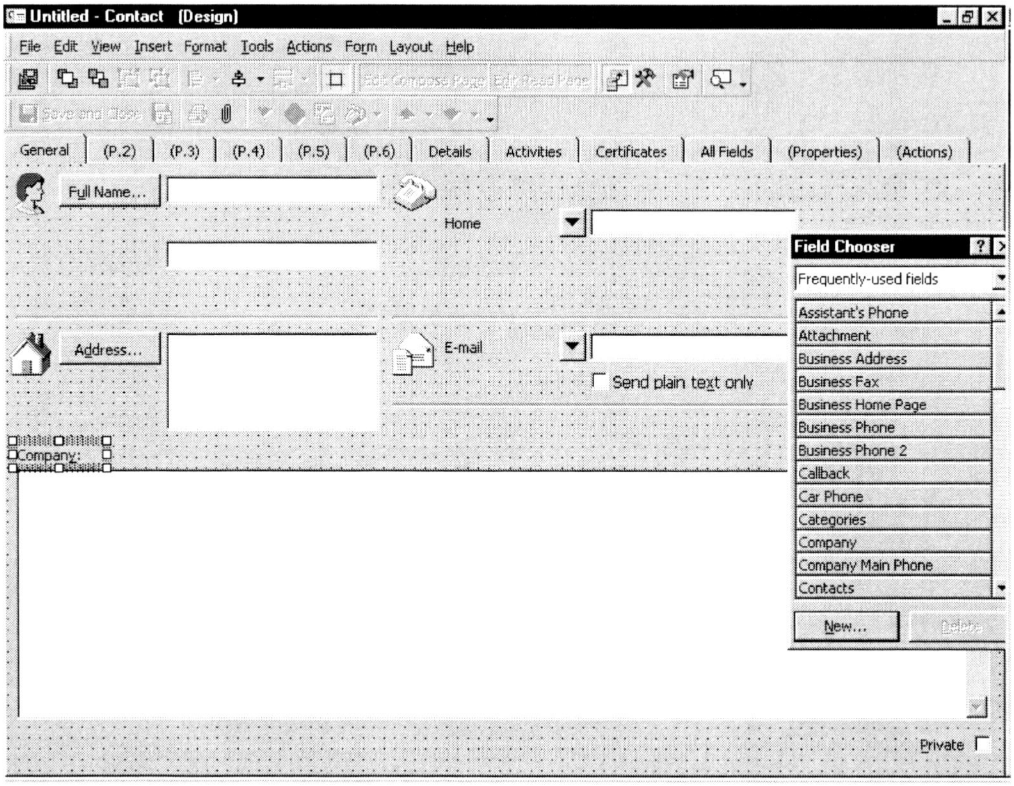

NEXT: Using the same method above, move the Home field, the drop-down arrow and text box up so that they are all on the same line as the Full Name field.

4. **Resize a field.**

CLICK: **Company**

THEN: Position the mouse pointer on the middle-right white box (called a *sizing handle*) of the Company box until it changes into a double-headed arrow ↔ (called a *size pointer*).

DRAG: The sizing handle to the right about 1".

5. **Rename a field.**

CLICK: In the box, select the text, and type **Customer Complaints:**

6. **Finish the form.**

FIRST: Delete the text box below the Full Name text box.

CLICK: The **Close**  button in the top-right corner of the Field chooser toolbar.

Your form should now look similar to the following:

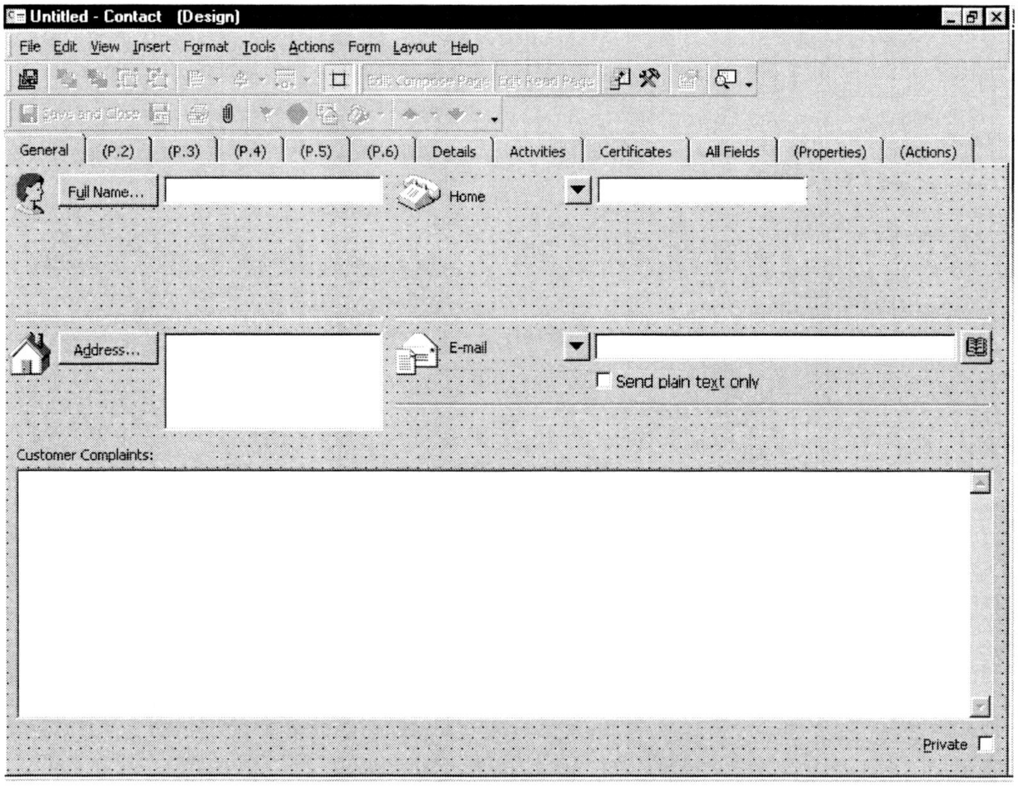

7. **Publish the form.**

CLICK: The **Publish Form**  button on the toolbar.

The Publish Form As dialog box is displayed.

CLICK: The Look In drop-down list and click **Contacts**.

CLICK: In the Display name text box and type **Guest**.

The Form name text box is automatically filled in for you.

CLICK: The **Publish** button.

The form is created.

THEN: Close the form without saving changes.

8. Use a custom form.

CLICK: **Actions** on the menu bar.

A new command called New Guest appears on the Actions menu.

CLICK: **New Guest**

A progress bar appears as the form is installed on your computer. (This will happen only once.) Then, the new form is displayed.

TYPE: **Michael James**

CLICK: In the Address text box and type: **2233 East Forest Lane**.

PRESS: **Enter**

TYPE: **Littleton, CO 80124**

CLICK: In the Home text box, and type **303-555-1234**

CLICK: In the E-mail text box, and type **mjames@isp.com**.

CLICK: In the Customer Complaints text box, and type **Didn't have soap in the bathroom**.

CLICK: The **Save and Close** button.

RIGHT-CLICK: A blank area of the Contacts list, click **Filter**, and click the **Clear All** button.

The guest is added to the contacts list as shown below:

TIP

You can delete the custom form by clicking **Tools** on the menu bar, and clicking **Options** on the Tools menu. Click the **Other** tab, click the **Advanced Options** button, click the **Custom Forms** button, and click the **Manage Forms** button. Then click the second **Set** button, click the plus sign to the left of the Personal Folders folder, and double-click the **Contacts** folder. Click the name of the form, if necessary, click the **Delete** button, and then click **Yes**. Close all open dialog boxes.

QuickLook at Lesson 5

To	Do This
Flag contacts for follow up	1. Select or open a contact. 2. Click the **Flag For Follow Up** button on the toolbar to display the Flag for Follow Up dialog box. 3. Click the Flag to drop-down arrow, and click an option *Or* Type an action. 4. Click the Due by drop-down arrow, and click a date. 5. Click **OK**.
Mark a flag as complete	1. Right-click the flagged contact. 2. Click **Flag Complete**.
Sort contacts	1. Click the column heading that you want to sort by to toggle between ascending and descending order. *Or* 1. Right-click a blank area of the contact list, and click **Sort** to display the Sort dialog box. 2. Click the Sort items by drop-down arrow, click an item, and click the **Ascending** or **Descending** option. 3. If desired, click the Then by drop-down arrow, click an item, and click the **Ascending** or **Descending** option. 4. If desired, to change the field sets displayed in the Sort items by and Then by lists, click the Select available fields from drop-down arrow, and click a new field set. 5. Click **OK**.
Add or remove fields in the current view	1. Right-click a blank area of the Contacts list. 2. Click **Show Fields**. 3. In the Show these fields in this order list, click a field, and click the **Remove** button. *Or* In the Available fields list, click a field, and click the **Add** button. 4. Repeat step 3 as necessary. 5. Click **OK**.

To	Do This
Use contacts to create mailing labels	1. Open the Contacts folder that you want to use. If desired, filter your contacts and/or select contacts. 2. Click **Tools** on the menu bar. 3. Click **Mail Merge** on the Tools menu to display the Mail Merge Contacts dialog box. 4. In the Contacts section, click the desired option. 5. In the Fields to merge section, click the desired option. 6. In the Document file section, click the desired option. 7. In the Contact data file section, click the desired option. 8. In the Merge options section, click the Document type drop-down arrow, and click **Mailing Labels**. Then click the merge to drop-down arrow, and click and option. 9. Click **OK**. 10. Click the Complete Setup option. 11. If an alert box appears, click **OK**. 12. Click the **Setup** button to display the Label Options dialog box. 13. Select options as desired. 14. Click **OK** to display the Create Labels dialog box. 15. Click the **Insert Merge Field** button, and select the first field name for the label. 16. Repeat the previous step until all the fields are entered. (Make sure you add any necessary spaces and punctuation.) 17. Click **OK**. 18. Click the **Merge** button. 19. In the Merge dialog box, click the **Merge** button. 20. Print and/or save the completed labels.

To	Do This
Create a custom form for contacts	**1.** Open a new contact window. **2.** Click **Tools** on the menu bar. **3.** Point to **Forms**. **4.** Click **Design This Form** to open the design window. **5.** If desired, click a tab on the form that you want to change. **6.** Make changes to the layout of the form by moving, resizing, adding, or deleting field labels and elements. **7.** When you are finished customizing the form, click the **Publish Form** button on the toolbar to display the Publish Form As dialog box. **8.** Click the Look In drop-down arrow, and click Contacts. **9.** Click in the Display name text box, and type a display name. **10.** Click the **Publish** button.
Access a custom form	**1.** Click **Actions** on the menu bar. **2.** Click **New [name of form]** on the Actions menu.

SkillCheck – Lesson 5

1. Flag the contact Ben Lynn to remind you to send him a birthday card next Monday.

2. Sort contacts in Phone List view by business phone in descending order.

3. Display only the contacts from Arizona.

4. Perform a mail merge, using the contacts in the current view, to create envelopes. Close the document window without saving.

5. Modify the Guest form you created earlier so that the large Customer Complaints box is half its size, and to the right of it there is another box the same size called Customer Comments. Call the modified Guest form Guest1.

Answers to the SkillChecks can be found here: **http://www.activeed.com/skanswers/outlook2.htm**

Performance Objectives

You will learn how to:

- Use the Journal to record a task
- Create and update recurring tasks
- Respond to task requests

USING THE JOURNAL TO RECORD A TASK

For Your Information

The *Journal* is a timeline folder that automatically records the creation, use, and modification of Office applications (Excel, Access, Word, and PowerPoint). You can also track various Outlook activities, such as e-mails, and tasks.

Recording a Task in the Journal

The Journal does not automatically track Outlook items, so if you want to track an Outlook item, you need to manually record it in the Journal.

The marketing manager at Lakewood Mountain Resort likes to record tasks in the Journal so that she can have a record of when she starts working on a particular task. She also likes to use the Journal to get a quick view of all the recorded items that she has been working on. If she wants to see a particular item, she opens it directly from within the Journal.

To record a task in the Journal:

1. Create a task.
2. Drag the task to the Journal folder.
3. Click the Save and Close button in the Journal Entry window.

To access an item in the Journal:

1. Display the Journal.
2. Right-click the item.
3. Click Open Item Referred To.

TRY IT 6–1 — RECORD A TASK IN THE JOURNAL

In this exercise, you will create a task and record it in the Journal. Then you will access the task from within the Journal and update it.

---

1. **Display the Tasks folder.**

2. **Create a task.**

   CLICK: The text *Click here to add a new Task.*

   TYPE: **Pick up brochures from the printer.**

   PRESS: **Enter**

   The task is created.

3. **Record a task in the Journal.**

   DRAG: The task *Pick up brochures from the printer* to the Journal folder on the Outlook bar.

   A Journal Entry window appears as shown below:

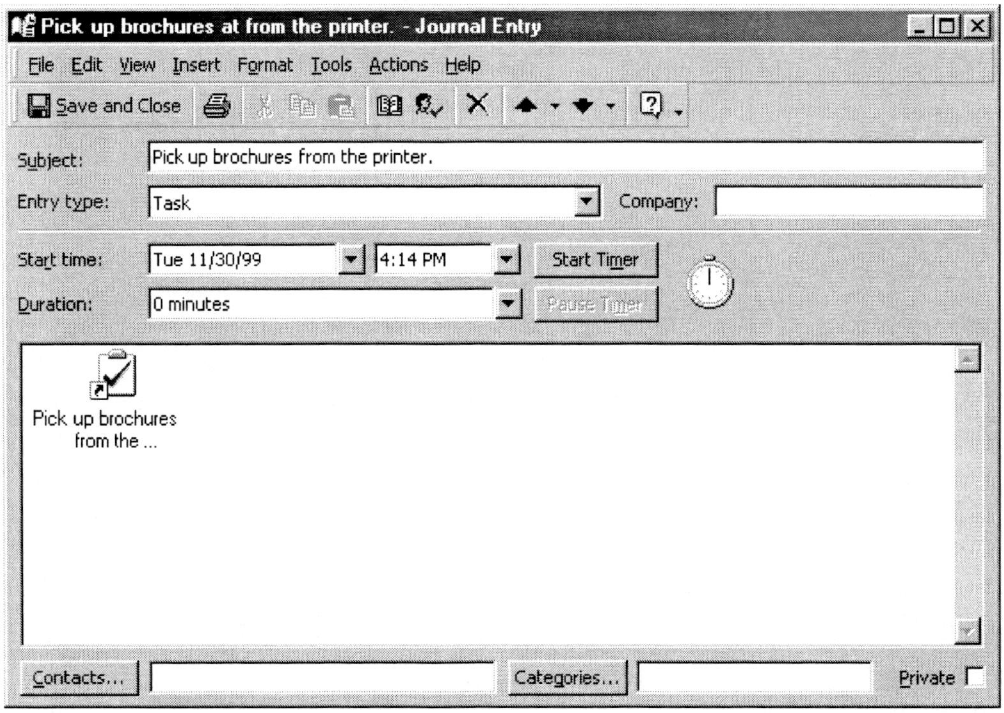

TIP

You can also record a task in the Journal by creating a task, selecting the task, clicking **Edit** on the menu bar, clicking **Copy to Folder**, if necessary, clicking the **Journal** folder, clicking **OK**, and clicking the **Save and Close** button.

TIP

You can manually record an activity in the Journal. Click **File** on the menu bar, point to **New** on the File menu, click **Journal Entry** on the New submenu. Type a subject, click the Entry type drop-down arrow to select an activity, select options as desired, and click the **Save and Close** button.

CLICK: The **Save and Close** button.

The task will now also appear in the Journal.

4. **Display the Journal.**

CLICK: The **Journal** icon on the Outlook bar.

THEN: If necessary, click the **Day** button on the toolbar.

The current day and the task appear in the Journal.

5. **Use the Journal to open the task.**

RIGHT-CLICK: The task.

CLICK: **Open Item Referred To**

The task is opened.

6. **Update the task.**

THEN: Select the **0** in the % Completed text box.

TYPE: **100**

CLICK: The **Save and Close** button.

The task is updated.

7. **Display the Tasks folder.**

Notice that the task is also update in the Tasks folder.

Creating and Updating Recurring Tasks

For Your Information

You can create a recurring task that occurs at any time you specifiy. Each time you complete the recurring task, you can update the Tasks folder by marking the task as complete.

Creating a Recurring Task

The restaurant manager at Lakewood Mountain Resort sends bi-weekly updates to the accounting department concerning any dinners that he decided to comp. To remind himself to do this, he created a recurring task called Comp Update.

You can customize the appearance of the menus and toolbars in the Tasks folder by right-clicking a toolbar or menu name and clicking Customize (the Customize dialog box will appear). On the Toolbars tab, you can add or remove toolbars. On the Commands tab, you can click a category in the Categories list, and drag a command onto a toolbar or menu. Conversely, you can drag a command off of the toolbar or menu when the Customize dialog box is displayed. Finally, on the Options tab, you can click the Reset my usage data button to restore the toolbar and menus to their default settings. You can also display the toolbar button with large icons, show shortcut keys in ScreenTips, turn on various menu animations, and turn off the options to list font names in their font and to show ScreenTips on toolbars.

To create a recurring task:

❶ Click the New Task button on the toolbar.

❷ Type a subject in the Subject text box.

❸ Select options as desired.

❹ Click the Recurrence button on the toolbar to display the Task Recurrence dialog box, shown on the next page.

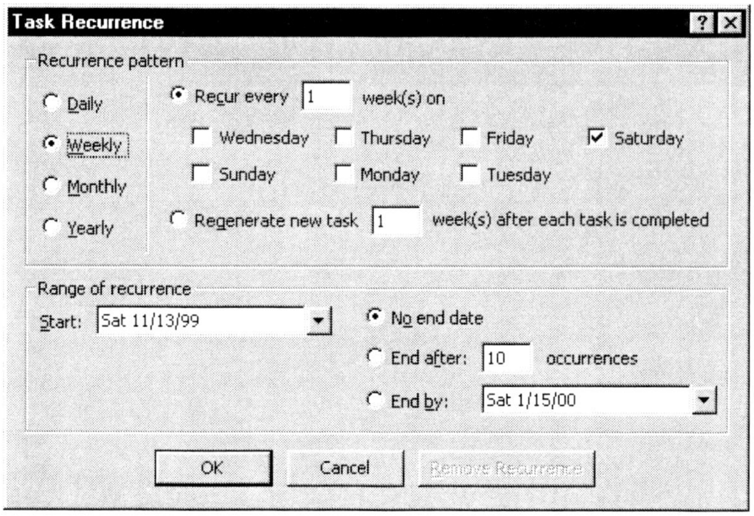

❺ Specify the recurrence pattern.

❻ Select desired options.

❼ Click OK.

❽ Click the Save and Close button on the toolbar.

Updating a Recurring Task

Each time the restaurant manager at Lakewood Mountain Resort sends an update to the accounting department, he updates the Tasks folder by marking the Comp Update task as completed.

To update a recurring task:

❶ Display the task list in Detailed List view.

❷ Click in the Status field of the recurring task to display a drop-down list.

❸ Click an item in the Status list.

Or

Select the text in the % Complete field, and type a new percent.

TRY IT 6–2 — CREATE AND UPDATE A RECURRING TASK

In this exercise, you will create a task called Comp Update that will recur every other Friday, and then you will update one of the tasks.

---

1. **Create a recurring task.**

CLICK: The **New Task** [New] button on the toolbar.

The Task window appears.

TYPE: **Comp Update** in the Subject text box.

CLICK: The Start date drop-down arrow, and click next Friday.

CLICK: The **Recurrence** button on the toolbar.

The Task Recurrence dialog box is displayed. Notice that the Weekly option is already selected.

THEN: Select the number **1** in the Recur every text box, and type **2**.

NEXT: If necessary, clear any check boxes that are selected other than Friday.

CLICK: **OK**

The Task window reappears with a message at the top describing that the tasks will be due every 2 weeks on Friday.

CLICK: The **Save and Close** button on the toolbar.

The recurring task is now displayed in the task list.

2. **Update the task.**

CLICK: **View** on the menu bar.

THEN: Point to **Current View** on the View menu.

CLICK: **Detailed List** on the Current View submenu.

The task list is displayed in the Detailed List view.

CLICK: The text *Not Started* in the Comp Update task.

A drop-down arrow and list are displayed.

TIP

You can also mark a task as complete by right-clicking the task, and clicking **Mark Complete**.

CLICK: **Completed**

CLICK: A blank area of the task list.

The message is crossed out and another Comp Update task appears with a due date two weeks later than the previous due date.

THEN: Select the text **0%** in the % Complete field of the new task.

TYPE: **5**

PRESS: **Enter**

The Status field of the new task now displays the text In Progress.

Accepting, Declining, and Reassigning Tasks

For Your Information

When you assign a task to another person, the person to whom you assign the task will receive a task request by e-mail. The recipient can accept, decline, or reassign the task to someone else.

Responding to a Task Request

After you send a task request, you will no longer be the owner of the task. You will not be able to change any information regarding the task, such as the task's due date. Unless you specify otherwise, Outlook will display a copy of the task in your task list, and when the person who accepted the task completes it, you will receive a status report.

If you are the recipient of a task request and accept the task, you become the owner of the task. If you decline a task, you can explain why you can't accept, and then the task is returned to the person who sent it. If you assign the task to another person, you do not become the owner of the task; however, you can choose to keep a copy of the task in your task list, and receive a status report when the task is completed.

To accept or decline a task:

> You must set your E-mail Services options to Internet Only to respond to and reassign task requests. (Display your Inbox, click Tools, click Options, click the Mail Services tab, and click the Reconfigure Mail Support button. In the dialog box, click the Internet Only option, click the Next button, and then follow the screen prompts.)

❶ Open the message that contains the task request.

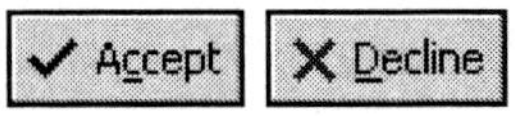

❷ Click the Accept button or click the Decline button.

❸ To accept or decline without typing a comment, click OK.

Or

To accept or decline with a comment, click the Edit the response before sending option, click OK, type a comment, and click the Send button.

❹ Close the message window.

To reassign a task to someone else:

❶ Open the message that contains the task request.

❷ Click the Assign Task button.

❸ In the To text box, type the e-mail address of the person you want to send the task to.

❹ Select or clear the Keep an updated copy of this task on my task list check box and the Send me a status report when this task is complete check box.

❺ Click the Send button.

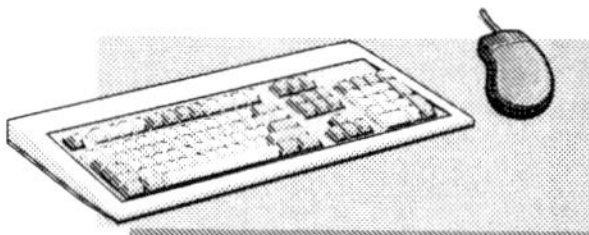

TRY IT 6–3 — RESPOND TO TASK REQUESTS

In this exercise, you will create two tasks and assign them to your class partner (your class partner will assign them to you as well). You will then accept and decline task requests.

---

1. Create the first task.

CLICK: The **New Task** button on the toolbar.

The Task window appears.

TIP

You can also create a task request by clicking the drop-down arrow to the right of the New Task button, and clicking **Task Request**.

TYPE: **File customer comments**

CLICK: The Due date drop-down arrow, and click tomorrow's date.

CLICK: The **Assign Task** 

button.

Another Task window appears.

CLICK: The **To** button.

The Select Task Recipient dialog box appears.

THEN: Scroll, if necessary, and click your class partner's name.

CLICK: The **To** button, and click **OK**.

Notice that the Keep an updated copy of this task on my task list check box and the Send me a status report when this task is complete check boxes are already selected. If the recipient accepts the task, you will receive a message that the task is completed.

CLICK: The **Send**  button.

An alert box appears, stating that because you are no longer the owner of the task, the task reminder has been shut off.

CLICK: **OK**

The task request is sent to your class partner, and the task appears in you task list.

2. **Create the second task.**

CLICK: The **New Task** button on the toolbar.

The Task window appears.

TYPE: **Send thank you cards to last month's guests**

CLICK: The Due date drop-down arrow, and click tomorrow's date.

CLICK: The **Assign Task**  button.

Another Task window appears.

CLICK: The **To** button.

The Select Task Recipient dialog box appears.

THEN: Scroll, if necessary, click your class partner's name, and click **OK**.

CLICK: The **Send**  button.

An alert box appears, stating that because you are no longer the owner of the task, the task reminder has been shut off.

CLICK: **OK**

The task request is sent to your class partner, and the task appears in you task list.

3. **Display the Inbox.**

4. **Manually send and receive task requests.**

CLICK: The **Send/Receive** button on the toolbar.

Your task requests are sent and your class partner's task request is sent to you.

5. **Accept a task.**

DOUBLE-
CLICK: The task request, **File customer comments**.

The task request is opened.

CLICK: The **Accept** 

button.

An alert box (shown below) appears, asking if you want to edit the response or send it as is. The Send the response now option is already selected.

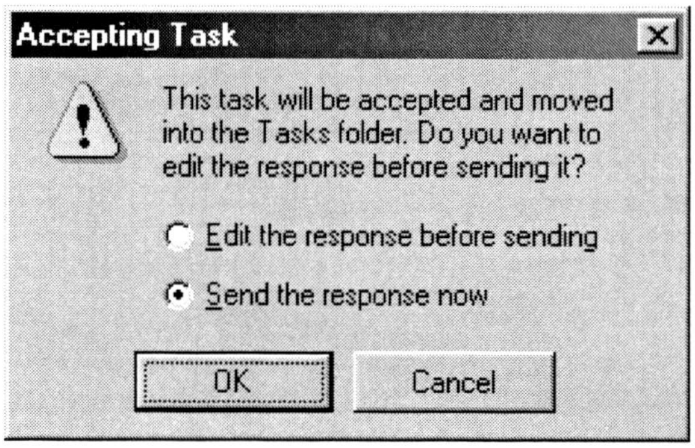

CLICK: **OK**

THEN: Close the message window.

The message is sent to your class partner.

6. **Mark the task "File customer comments" (which your class partner sent to you) as completed, and click the Send/Receive button.**

A status report is sent to your class partner, stating that the task has been completed.

If you open and close the status report, then display your Tasks folder, the task will also be marked as completed in your task list.

7. Decline a task.

FIRST: Display the Inbox.

DOUBLE-CLICK: The task request, **Send thank you cards to last month's guests**.

The task request is opened.

CLICK: The **Decline** [X Decline] button.

The Declining Task alert box appears.

CLICK: The Edit the response before sending option.

CLICK: **OK**

TYPE: **I cannot accept this task because I'm too busy.**

Your message window should look like the following figure:

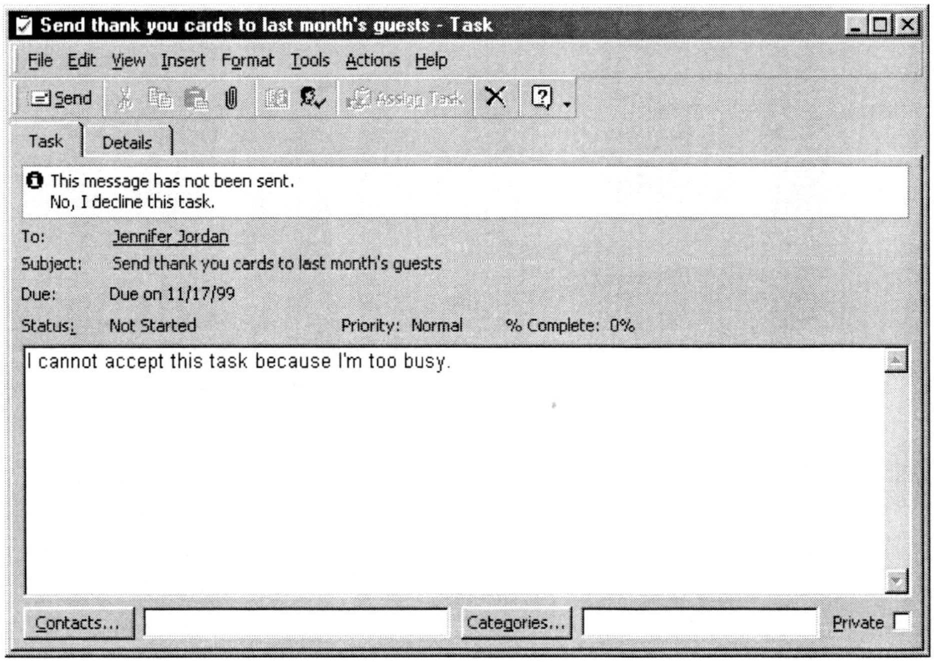

CLICK: The **Send** [Send] button.

The message is sent to your class partner.

QuickLook at Lesson 6

To	Do This
Record a task in the Journal	**1.** Create a task. **2.** Drag the task to the Journal folder. **3.** Click the **Save and Close** button.
Access an item in the Journal	**1.** Display the Journal. **2.** Right-click the item. **3.** Click **Open Item Referred To**.
Create a recurring task	**1.** Click the **New Task** button on the toolbar. **2.** Type a subject in the Subject text box. **3.** Select options as desired. **4.** Click the **Recurrence** button on the toolbar to display the Task Recurrence dialog box. **5.** Specify the recurrence pattern. **6.** Select desired options. **7.** Click **OK**. **8.** Click the **Save and Close** button on the toolbar.
Update a recurring task	**1.** Display the task list in Detailed List view. **2.** Click in the Status field of the recurring task to display a drop-down list. **3.** Click an item in the Status list. *Or* Select the text in the % Complete field, and type a new percent.
Accept or decline a task	**1.** Open the message that contains the task request. **2.** Click the **Accept** button or click the **Decline** button. **3.** To accept or decline without typing a comment, click **OK**. *Or* To accept or decline with a comment, click the Edit the response before sending option, click **OK**, type a comment, and then click the **Send** button. **4.** Close the message window.

To	Do This
Reassign a task to someone else	**1.** Open the message that contains the task request. **2.** Click the **Assign Task** button. **3.** In the **To** text box, type the e-mail address of the person you want to send the task to. **4.** Select or clear the Keep an updated copy of this task on my task list check box and the Send me a status report when this task is complete check box. **5.** Click the **Send** button.

SkillCheck – Lesson 6

1. Create a task using the following information:

Description	Information
Subject	Buy party supplies for company party
Due date	One week from today

2. Record the task in the Journal.

3. Create a recurring task using the following information:

Description	Information
Subject	Feed sister's cat while she's on vacation.
Start date	Next Tuesday
Recurrence pattern	Every Tuesday and Thursday for the next four weeks

4. Mark the first and second occurrences of the recurring task as completed.

5. Assign a task to your class partner using the following information:

Description	Information
Subject	Send out invitations to company party
Due date	Tomorrow

6. Manually send and receive messages.

7. After you receive the task request from your class partner, reassign the task to a person in your class (other than your class partner).

Answers to the SkillChecks can be found here: **http://www.activeed.com/skanswers/outlook2.htm**

You will learn how to:

- Set up the Fax Service
- Create and send faxes
- Receive faxes

USING FAX SERVICES IN OUTLOOK

For Your Information

You can use Outlook to create, send, and receive faxes. In order to this, you must first install Microsoft Fax. The steps to install Microsoft will vary depending on which version of Windows you are using and whether you have your e-mail service setup for Internet Only or Corporate or Workgroup.

Setting Up

If you installed a Corporate or Workgroup e-mail service, you must install Microsoft Fax from Windows, add it to your mail profile, and then reinstall Office 2000.

If you installed an Internet Only e-mail service, you will install the Symantec Fax Starter Edition as an add-in component.

To install Microsoft Fax with a Corporate or Workgroup installation from Windows 95:

1. Click Start.
2. Point to Settings, and then click Control Panel.
3. Double-click Add/Remove Programs.
4. On the Windows Setup tab, click Microsoft Fax.
5. Click OK.

To install Microsoft Fax with a Corporate or Workgroup installation from the Windows 98 CD-ROM:

1. Insert the Windows 98 CD-ROM.
2. In the Exploring window, display your CD-ROM drive, and navigate to tools\OldWin95\message\us
3. Double-click the file Awfax.exe to install the fax.

After you install Microsoft fax, you must add it to your mail profile.

To add Microsoft Fax to your mail profile:

1. Click Start.
2. Point to Settings and click Control Panel.
3. Double-click the Mail (or Mail and Fax) icon.
4. Click Add.
5. Click Microsoft Fax.
6. Click OK.

   Microsoft Fax is added to your mail profile. You must now reinstall Office 2000.

7. Click Start.
8. Point to Settings and click Control Panel.
9. Double-click the Add/Remove Programs icon.
10. On the Install/Uninstall tab, click Microsoft Office 2000.
11. Click Add/Remove.
12. Click Repair Office.
13. Click Reinstall Office 2000.
14. Click Finish.

After you install the Microsoft Fax, you will be prompted to enter some basic information regarding your location and phone number. You will need a fax number and a modem.

To install the Fax Service with an Internet Only installation:

1. Click Start.
2. Point to Settings, and click Control Panel.
3. Double-click Add/Remove Programs.
4. Click Microsoft Office 2000.

5. Click Add/Remove.

6. Click Add Or Remove Features.

7. Click the plus sign to the left of Microsoft Outlook for Windows to show the installation options.

8. Click the icon next to Symantec Fax Starter Edition, and click Run From My Computer.

9. Click Update Now.

10. After Symantec Fax Starter Edition is installed, start Outlook, and follow the steps in the Symantec Fax Starter Edition Setup Wizard.

> If the Symantec Fax Starter Edition Setup Wizard does not start, close Outlook and run Olfsetup.exe. Click Start, point to Find, and click Files Or Folders. In the Named box, type Olfsetup.exe. In the Look In list, click your hard disk. Select the Include Subfolders check box, and click Find Now. When the file name is displayed in the lower pane, double-click it to start the Symantec Fax Starter Edition Setup Wizard.

Creating and Sending a Fax

When you create a fax you can choose to send only a cover sheet that has a message on it, send a cover sheet and any attached files, or just send files without a cover sheet.

You can create your own cover sheet or use one of Microsoft Fax's four cover sheets: Confidential!, For your information, Generic, or Urgent! To view the different types of cover sheets, click Tools on the menu bar, point to Microsoft Fax Tools, and click Options. On the Message tab in the Default cover page section, click one of the cover pages in the list and click Open. Microsoft Fax will open the cover sheet. You will notice that generic names such as "Sender's Company" and "Sender's Address." When you actually send the cover sheet, Microsoft Fax will put your information in these spots in place of the generic text. (This will depend on what information you have on the User tab in the Microsoft Fax Properties dialog box. To view this information, click Tools on the menu bar, point to Microsoft Fax Tools, click Options, and click the User tab.)

To create and send a Fax:

1. Click Actions on the menu bar.
2. Click New Fax Message on the Actions menu to display the Compose New Fax Wizard.
3. Select desired options and click Next.
4. In the To text box, type the name of the person that you are going to send the fax to.
5. In the Fax # text box, type your contact's fax number.
6. If desired, click the Add to List button.
7. Click Next.
8. Specify whether you want to use a cover page. If you do, select the type of cover page in the list.
9. Click Next.
10. Type a subject.
11. If desired, type a note.
12. Click Next.
13. If you want to include any files in the fax, click the Add File button.
14. Navigate to the location and click Open.
15. Click Next.
16. Click Finish.

You can customize a fax by clicking Tools on the menu bar, pointing to Microsoft Fax Tools, and clicking Options. On the Message tab, click the Add button in the Default cover page section. If necessary, close the Cover Page Editor Tips dialog box. Use the buttons on the Drawing toolbar to create a custom cover page. When you are finished, save the cover sheet, using a name of your choice, and close it. When you send a fax, click the name of your custom fax in the Compose New Fax Wizard.

Receiving a Fax

Any faxes that you receive will appear in your Inbox. Fax will automatically appear, or you can manually receive them.

To manually receive a fax:

❶ Click Tools on the menu bar.

❷ Point to Send/Receive.

❸ Click Microsoft Fax.

GLOSSARY

NOTE: Words that appear in bold within definitions indicate terms that are also defined in this glossary.

Address book	List of contacts' e-mail addresses. An address can be automatically inserted into a new message window in the To text box, so that you don't have to manually address the e-mail message.
Appointment	An activity that you schedule in Outlook for yourself.
Archive	A backup copy of one or more Outlook folders; the process of moving old messages into a folder on your hard disk.
Category	A keyword or phrase that you can use to find, sort, filter, or group items.
Clipboard	An area in your computer's memory that temporarily stores content when you cut or copy text and graphics.
Data source	The file in a mail merge that contains information that varies, such as information about each contact in your Contacts folder.
Delegate access	Authorization for someone to send or maintain Outlook items on your behalf.
Event	An activity that has a 24 hour or longer duration, such as a seminar or a vacation.
Fields	The categories in the data source that will be inserted into the main document during the merge process.
Filter	The process of narrowing a search with specified criteria; a program that takes data, transforms it, and then outputs the transformed data.
Flag	The act of marking a contact to remind yourself to perform an action, such as call or e-mail the contact; the symbol that appears next to the contact's name when it has been marked for an action.
Folder List	Contains public and personal folders available in Outlook.
HTML	The markup language that is used to display documents on the Internet.

iCalendar (Internet Calendar)	A component of Outlook that allows you to share whether you are free or busy at certain times of the day with people over the Internet.
Journal	A timeline folder that automatically records the creation, use, and modification of Office applications, and tracks various Outlook activities such as e-mails and tasks.
Main document	A file used in mail merge that contains fixed text, such as the body of a form letter.
Meeting	A type of appointment you invite others to attend. Prospective attendees can accept or decline the invitation.
Net Folder	A folder that is shared over the Internet with subscribed users.
Newsgroup	A collection of messages, related in subject, that are constantly being sent and responded to by people belonging to the group.
News server	A computer that is maintained by a company, group, or individual, and is configured to accept messages from newsgroups.
Offline	When Outlook is not connected to the server.
Online	When Outlook is connected to the server.
OST file	A folder file that contains copies of all of your Outlook folders, which is used track **offline** and **online** folders.
Permission	Authorization granted to another user to access Outlook folders.
Personal distribution list	A collection of contacts (who have something in common, such as they all work in the same department) used to send a message to everyone named on the list.
Public folder	A folder that contains messages or information that can be shared with designated users.
Publish	The process of sharing a **Net Folder** with specific people over the Internet; the process of adding a new form to Outlook; to display a Web page on the Internet.
Read receipt	A notice (in the form of an e-mail) that tells you that a message was received and read by a recipient.

Recurring appointment An activity, scheduled in the Calendar, that occurs at multiple times or at regular intervals.

Restore The process of returning archived items to Outlook.

Roles Levels of involvement that are assigned to a network user.

Rule A set of conditions, actions, and exceptions that when enforced, processes and organizes e-mail messages in a certain way.

Rules Wizard A wizard that allows you to set conditions that will automatically perform actions on e-mail messages.

Signature A text message attached to the end of a message that contains personal information about the sender.

Subscriber A person who is granted permission to a **Net Folder**.

Synchronize The ability of Outlook to compare files created offline to the corresponding files that are online and then change the online files to match the offline files.

Task Either a personal or work item to be completed. A task can be assigned to other network users.

Template In Outlook, an item, such as an e-mail message, that can be used as a pattern to format similar items.

vCard An attachment that contains contact information in the form of an electronic business card.

Windows NetMeeting A program that enables you to conduct real-time meetings over the Internet.

INDEX

Note: Boldfaced numbers indicate pages in TRY IT exercises. Italicized page numbers indicate illustrations.

A

B

C

D

E

F

G

H

I

J

L

M

N

O

U

V

W